Contents

Foreword

Assessors and verifiers are critical to the future credibility, integrity and marketability of N/SVQs. In December 2001 the revised national occupational standards for assessment and verification were approved, and heralded a new era for assessors and verifiers, with a much clearer focus on quality assurance. ENTO developed the revised standards through extensive consultation with practitioners throughout the UK, who were also consulted on the development of this publication.

This guide is designed to be a definitive point of reference for assessors and verifiers. It gives authoritative advice on key issues relating to the assessment and verification processes. It has been developed to provide you, the practitioner, with practical hints and tips as well as case studies taken from accredited centres across a range of sectors. It also sets out to help you reduce bureaucracy in the system.

The publication has been written by Hilary Read, a renowned author and trainer in the sector, with expert critique from Bridget Herniman and Sally Garbett, both respected practitioners and trainers on issues relating to assessment and verification.

I trust that you will find this publication a useful source of reference to support your development as an assessor and verifier. Ultimately, the quality of assessment and verification of competence has an impact on the individual being assessed and – where the assessment leads to accreditation – the marketability of that qualification. Our challenge is to ensure that all candidates gaining an N/SVQ have a qualification that is respected and valued by employers and, more importantly, by the candidates themselves. Excellence in assessment and verification *will provide you with the information you need to meet this challenge.*

David Morgan
Director, ENTO

COLEG SIR GAR	
Dawson	21-11-05
	25 - 00
AM/12/06/013	-

Introduction

This guide is for everyone involved in the assessment or verification of Scottish or National Vocational Qualifications (SVQs or NVQs). If you are new to assessing or verifying, it will help you get to grips with all aspects of your job and to understand where you fit within the bigger picture of learning and development. If you are an experienced assessor or verifier, you will find help with recent changes to assessor and verifier standards and suggestions for updating and improving your practice.

The guide has been written for:

■ *assessors of NVQs and work-based learning programmes.*

■ *internal verifiers: all those with responsibility to quality assure, manage, deliver or train within NVQ programmes.*

The structure of the guide

This guide has the following sections:

Introduction
This explains the principles underpinning the guide.

1 Verification: a management role
This explains the role of the internal verifier, and concentrates on the main aspects of the verifier's job in:

- managing and quality assuring the delivery of NVQs

- managing, supporting and developing staff

- verifying assessments.

2 Assessment: part of the learning process
This looks at the role of the assessor in identifying and accrediting learners' levels of competence.

3 Keeping records
This gives help with the different types of assessment documentation.

4 Getting qualified
This gives information about the qualifications you can gain if you work in work-based learning and development.

Further information
This section explains terminology and acronyms commonly used within the field of assessment and verification.

Where the guide refers to NVQs, this includes SVQs. The guide takes account of the new national standards and their associated assessment strategies for assessors and verifiers, and draws your attention to the regulations contained in the NVQ Code of Practice and their implications for providers of NVQs. For SVQs, please refer to the Guide to Assessment and Quality Assurance for Training Providers and Employers (SQA, March 2003).

Throughout this guide, you'll find examples of good practice taken from assessors and verifiers working within a range of organisations. Their experience will provide you with ideas for practical methods of working based on real-life situations, as well as helping you to identify areas for change within your own organisation.

Where do assessment and verification fit?

To ensure that you are delivering training and accrediting qualifications in line with national standards and regulations, enabling learners to be successful in achieving their chosen qualifications, you need a reliable system of assessment and verification. Assessors and verifiers play a key role in assessing learning and helping learners to progress, while ensuring that national standards of competence are maintained. As an assessor or verifier, you need to be clear about the part you play in enabling learners to succeed. Once you know the basics, you should be aiming to improve the quality of your assessment or verification practice.

Delivering assessment

Knowing when to assess is vital. It is expensive to assess learners before they have acquired the necessary skills and knowledge to perform consistently to the standards at work. It is therefore important for assessors to know how individual learners are progressing so that they can begin to plan for final (summative) assessment at the right time.

When you look at how learning and assessment are delivered, you can see how closely the two are linked, as follows:

Stage	Learning and development	Assessment
1 Recruitment	The learner is recruited to the programme.	The learner undergoes initial assessment to: - assess their potential - see what they can do already - gauge their suitability and is then registered with the awarding body.
2 Induction	The learner is inducted into their learning and development programme.	The learner is inducted into the NVQ or award.
3 Planning for learning and formative assessment	The learner agrees learning targets and plans how these will be achieved. These are recorded on an individual learning plan (ILP) or similar.	The results of initial assessment inform plans and ensure that realistic targets are set. Regular, formative assessment is planned.
4 Learning and development	The learner undergoes training/development over time and: - acquires skills and knowledge - practises what they have learned - applies what they have learned in the workplace - starts to perform to the standards - consistently performs to the standards under a variety of conditions at work.	Formative assessment takes place at regular intervals to see how the learner is progressing. Learners are given feedback on their performance, targets are adjusted and further training and development are arranged as necessary. When (and *only* when) the learner is performing confidently and consistently to national standards …
5 Assessment planning		… does planning for summative (final) assessment against the standards take place.
6 Summative assessment	If the learner is assessed as 'not yet competent', they may need to undertake further training or practice.	The assessor makes an assessment decision and gives feedback to the learner on their performance.
7 Certification		The learner receives a certificate of their achievement from the relevant awarding body.

The verification process

Ultimately, it is the internal verifier's job to ensure the integrity and quality of the awards, and so he or she must make sure that effective procedures and resources are in place to allow this to happen.

Here's how the verification process supports the delivery of assessment:

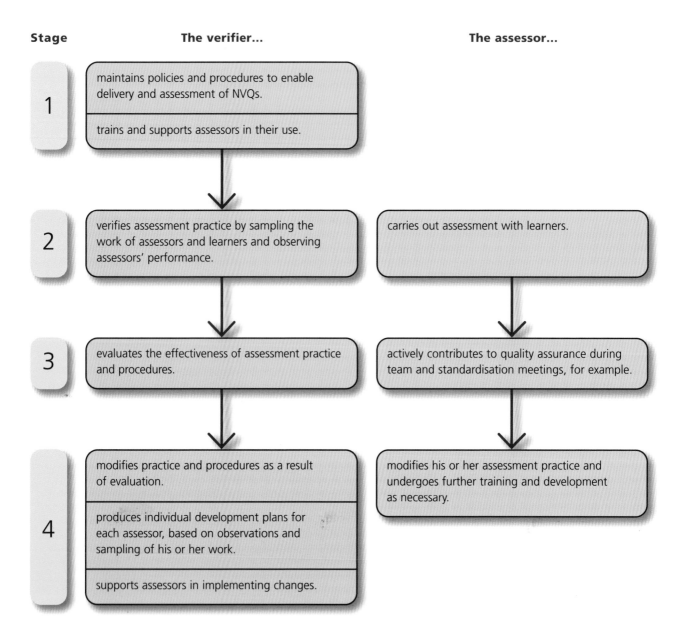

Stage	The verifier...	The assessor...
1	maintains policies and procedures to enable delivery and assessment of NVQs. / trains and supports assessors in their use.	
2	verifies assessment practice by sampling the work of assessors and learners and observing assessors' performance.	carries out assessment with learners.
3	evaluates the effectiveness of assessment practice and procedures.	actively contributes to quality assurance during team and standardisation meetings, for example.
4	modifies practice and procedures as a result of evaluation. / produces individual development plans for each assessor, based on observations and sampling of his or her work. / supports assessors in implementing changes.	modifies his or her assessment practice and undergoes further training and development as necessary.

National standards and the NVQ Code of Practice

National standards for assessment and verification form an integral part of the learning and development (L&D) qualifications structure. These qualifications are aimed at those responsible for work-based learning, assessment and verification.

You need to hold a recognised qualification yourself or be working towards one before you can start assessing or verifying NVQs.

Assessment and verification units are as follows:

Unit	Title		Aimed at...
A1	Assess learners using a range of methods	→	The assessor
V1	Conduct internal quality assurance of the assessment process	→	The internal verifier
V2	Conduct external quality assurance of the assessment process	→	The external verifier

These units form part of wider NVQs and certificate awards in learning and development. To see how roles and responsibilities are linked to the standards for assessors and verifiers or if you would like more information on gaining a qualification, turn to section 4, 'Getting qualified' (page 69).

The Qualifications and Curriculum Authority (QCA) has published the NVQ Code of Practice for all those involved in the delivery of NVQs in England, Wales and Northern Ireland (QCA, 2002). The code sets out:

- the processes and procedures you need in place within your centre to ensure high standards of assessment and verification across all the NVQs you offer

- external quality procedures for awarding bodies, including those aimed at external verifiers

- sanctions to be applied if you fail to meet the principles and procedures set out in the code. These range from entry into an action plan to withdrawal of centre approval if you fail to comply.

Key principles

There are five key principles that underpin good practice in assessment and verification. They form the central themes of this guide.

1 Verifiers need to have complete confidence in their assessors, the assessment process and in those providing administrative support within their schemes.

2 Effective verification is about setting up, implementing and maintaining quality-assurance procedures.

3 All assessors contribute to the quality-assurance process.

This means:

- having effective management and quality-assurance procedures in place

- ensuring that the right people who are occupationally competent are recruited and trained to carry out their roles

- knowing that assessors, verifiers and managers are committed to the NVQ processes and to maintaining the quality and integrity of awards within their centre.

This means:

- giving the internal verifier the scope and authority within the organisation that reflects this responsibility and enables him or her to carry out the job

- carrying out initial benchmarking and data collection and analysis before putting appropriate strategies and procedures into place

- having the verification process in place right at the start of the learning cycle, so that effective assessment can occur. It is the verifier's responsibility to have the right procedures to begin with, including the staff to deliver, and appropriate recruitment practices for learners

- creating a formal internal verification strategy that defines management, quality assurance and delivery procedures for each scheme.

This means:

- assessors need to know about the quality-assurance process and the part they play in improving the quality of assessment within the centre

- assessors need to attend team and standardisation meetings and take an active part in the process.

4 As well as assessing, assessors contribute to learning and development: they need to understand the part they play.

5 Assessors need to feel competent and confident about the judgements they make.

This means:

- ensuring that the right learner is on the right programme so as to maximise the chances of success. This is all down to effective recruitment and induction procedures and the assessor's ability to identify the support needs of individual learners

- knowing when and how to use effective initial, formative and summative assessment

- recognising and recording assessors' contributions to the learning process. Many assessors train or coach learners as part of their role, particularly when giving feedback on performance, but their contribution to learners' programmes or learning targets is often unintentional, unrecognised and unrecorded

- making sure that summative assessment happens at the right time – when the learner is working to the desired standard. In other words, you shouldn't be assessing in the early stages of learners' programmes unless it's to find out what they can already do or to review their progress. (The first part of any learning and development programme is about the learner acquiring and applying knowledge and practising skills, so the assessor will be carrying out formative assessment to ensure that the learner is on track with their learning.)

This means:

- being able to judge evidence from a variety of sources, using the most appropriate assessment methods for each learner

- being able to justify any assessment decision they make, and to feel comfortable and confident in doing so

- seeing the workplace as a rich source of both learning opportunities and performance evidence

- keeping effective records of their work so that others can audit the planning and decision-making processes.

Who does what

Here are the roles and responsibilities of all those working within assessment and verification.

The learner

This is the candidate for the NVQ and the person undertaking the work-based learning programme. He or she works in partnership with the assessor, and is responsible for:

- agreeing learning targets and working towards them

- being involved in the planning of their assessment activities

- submitting valid, authentic, current and sufficient evidence for assessment.

The learner becomes a candidate for the NVQ or award once they have been registered with an awarding body by their centre.

The assessor

This person is responsible for assessing the NVQ. The assessor works with the candidate in the following ways:

- inducting the candidate into the NVQ and explaining what needs to be done

- identifying any additional support requirements

- setting and modifying learning targets

- planning assessments

- undertaking a range of assessment activities

- providing constructive feedback to the candidate concerning his or her competence and progress

- recording assessments

- reviewing progress

- ensuring that the candidate has submitted enough evidence to allow internal verification to be carried out effectively.

Assessors are also responsible for:

- maintaining their own technical and vocational competencies in the areas that they are assessing

- contributing to the quality-assurance procedures within their centre.

The internal verifier

This is the person responsible for ensuring quality and consistency of assessment within the approved NVQ centre.

He or she works with assessors, and is responsible for:

- guiding and supporting assessors

- monitoring and assessing assessors' development and practice

- conducting formative (interim) and summative internal verification

- monitoring candidate records, progress and achievements

- working closely with the centre manager on the development of the centre's systems, procedures and staff competence

- conducting standardisation meetings within each occupational area

- conducting assessor or delivery team meetings

- answering all queries relating to the assessment and verification process

- supporting assessors in specific ways – such as providing for simulations and special needs.

Additional managerial responsibilities

In addition to the above, the internal verifier is responsible for contributing towards:

- staff retention and recruitment

- staffing levels and structures: allocation of internal verifiers to assessors and allocation of learners to assessors

- overseeing the effective running of the centre team(s)

- meeting awarding body requirements

- ensuring that centre policies and procedures are adhered to, and monitored and evaluated on a regular basis

- tracking and monitoring learners' progress

- providing support meetings for staff and learners

- providing administrative support to all staff and learners

- storing and recording completed awards for the verification process

- candidate induction packs

- specifying assessors' and internal verifiers' job roles

- standards and documentation

- dealing with appeals and problems with learners, their line managers or staff!

- providing resources for staff training and development.

The external verifier

The external verifier represents the awarding body. This person is responsible for assuring the quality of the assessment process across centres of all types. Their job also involves:

- reviewing a centre's assessment and verification methods; administration and recording arrangements; assessor selections; induction and support; standardisation; safety, equality and access arrangements; and internal evaluation

- checking staff competence and experience

- checking assessor support and standardisation

- sampling assessor judgements with learners

- giving feedback to centres in the form of written and verbal information and support, and clarifying issues and concerns

- completing appropriate monitoring reports

- taking part in appropriate updating/standardisation events

- meeting with learners

- providing advice and guidance to centres.

1 Verification: a management role

Internal verifiers have a management role: they are responsible for setting up and monitoring procedures and for the work of assessors and others such as administrative staff. As the verifier, your key to effective internal verification is to create and implement strategies that you review and evaluate on a regular basis.

This section concentrates on the three main areas of responsibility for the verifier, namely:

- *setting up and managing quality assurance*

- *training and supporting assessors*

- *verifying (quality assuring) the assessment process.*

As the internal verifier within your centre, you are leading a proactive process of quality management that enables both you and your assessors to accredit competence efficiently within the workplace. In other words, qualified professionals are assessing real workers in actual working environments within an overall operational framework of quality assurance (QA).

Verifying as quality assurance

Within the learning and development units, verification is described as 'internal quality assurance of the assessment process.'

In practice, this part of your job involves:

- **designing strategies, systems and procedures** that maintain the quality of assessment within your centre, monitoring these to see that they work in practice, and changing them if they don't

- **putting the right staffing structures and appropriate resources in place** to deliver assessment and verification

- **managing relationships and communications with those responsible for internal and external quality assurance** – your team, the external verifier and the awarding body.

Setting up a QA system

Your aim as internal verifier is continually to improve the quality of assessment and verification within your centre. You can use the QA cycle to help you do this. The cycle looks like the diagram below.

You keep going round the cycle as you plan, monitor, evaluate and reset your objectives as a result. In this way you can achieve continual improvement.

First, though, you need to know how you measure up so that you can formulate a plan and set yourself some objectives. You need to ask yourself: how effective are current management, quality assurance and delivery procedures within my centre or scheme?

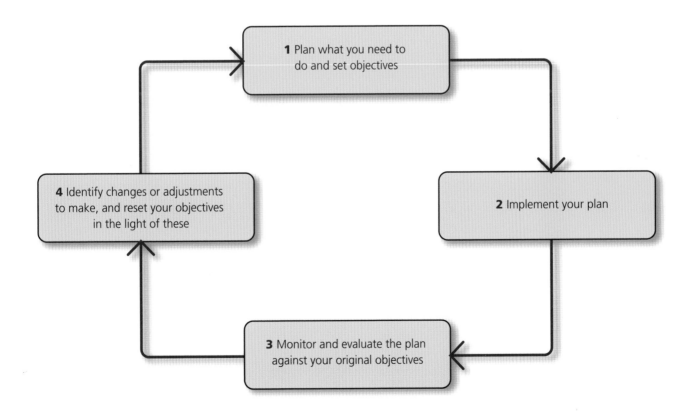

Establishing a starting point

To benchmark their current provision, the National Construction College used criteria within the NVQ Code of Practice and the requirements of the new occupational standards for assessors and internal verifiers. This gave them a starting point for action, as the following extracts from their audit show. (Other areas audited by the National Construction College include planning, management structures, resources, monitoring and reviewing, and records).

Criteria	What's happening now	What needs to happen
1 Centre's aims and policies are cascaded and understood by the whole team.	Staffing structures and procedures are being redone. Currently being drafted: ■ Procedures for internal verification ■ Assessment process ■ Equal opportunities policy ■ Appeals process ■ Health and Safety policy ■ Job descriptions for internal verifier and assessor.	Include organisation's equal opportunities policy in candidate and staff induction packs. All learners to sign that they have received and read policies and procedures at induction. Allocate one member of staff to field candidate concerns. Keep records of all candidate concerns. Carry out evaluations with learners at the following stages: ■ after induction ■ three-monthly ■ on leaving the programme. Statistics to be collected and analysed by the IV/QA team. Allocate learners to assessors. Develop new IT system to track candidate progress. Develop monthly tracking sheets for assessors to use.
2 Candidate's access to fair assessment policy and practice is understood and complied with by the whole team.	Candidate handbook is being written.	Candidate induction packs need to contain: ■ all policies and procedures ■ information about the relevant NVQ ■ what assessment means ■ names of staff who will be working with them and their roles. Packs to be piloted with existing learners.
3 Staff roles and responsibilities are clearly understood and complied with.	All job descriptions are being revisited.	Packs to be developed: ■ IV induction pack ■ Assessor induction pack. Allocate a centre co-ordinator, define role, draft induction pack and induct into the role.

Auditing provision

When setting up a QA system for assessment and verification, Loughborough College used the following six-phase plan:

Phase 1: Audit provision against the criteria within the QCA Code of Practice and the occupational standards for assessors and verifiers.

Phase 2: Produce a detailed report and development plan as a result of the audit.

Phase 3: Upskill internal verifiers.

Phase 4: Upskill assessors.

Phase 5: Design a scheme of work to enable assessors to gain A1 standards.

Phase 6: Design a scheme of work to enable verifiers to gain V1 standards.

The college's consultant, Bridget Herniman explains:

'Once you've completed phases 1 and 2, you've got your systems and procedures in place to support the delivery of the NVQs, so now you are in a position to train and support the staff. Some organisations try and do it the other way round and come unstuck. It's no good throwing good money into training unless you've specified what you're trying to do in the first place. You need the whole system up and running before you start training your staff.'

See the Appendix on page 79 for an audit tool that you can adapt and use to audit your own organisation.

Internal verification (IV) policies and strategies

Planning for quality assurance means that all those involved in assessment and verification know what's happening and the part they play. For this, you need a formal strategy for internal verification within your organisation that sets out your overall policy and explains procedures.

Your IV policy

This is your 'statement of intent for internal verification' across the whole of your organisation. It is aimed at all staff involved in the delivery, co-ordination, management and administration of NVQs. If you are a large centre offering different NVQs, your policy should cover *all* schemes.

The policy should describe:

- **your organisational structure:** roles, responsibilities and job descriptions for carrying out assessment and internal verification
- **a description of the process of internal verification:** what happens and when, including any internal quality-assurance objectives you have set within the centre
- **supporting documentation** for generic recording of the IV process, and delivery of NVQs to meet your QA measures or objectives set within the centre (these can be referred to in appendices if necessary)
- **monitoring and management procedures:** details of how the performance of those involved in delivery is to be monitored and managed, and the ways in which you propose to do this.

Other procedures

You also need to ensure that you have formal procedures for dealing with:

- appeals and complaints
- equal opportunities
- data protection and candidate confidentiality
- bullying and harassment
- health and safety.

Your IV strategies

Each NVQ scheme needs a specific strategy that sets out clearly its management, quality assurance and delivery. If you don't have detailed strategies, you will need to create them and modify them for each scheme.

Each strategy should contain:

- **an overview of the NVQ assessment strategy**, and how you plan to meet and deliver it. Assessment strategies are developed by professional organisations such as your sector skills council, former NTO or standards-setting body, which are responsible for developing national occupational standards contained within the NVQs, describing how these should be delivered and by whom.

  You should also include examples of any documentation you plan to use or that your awarding body requires you to complete.

- **names and job titles of team members:** all those involved in the delivery of the scheme, including relevant details of their competence to deliver, assess or verify.

- **management of the team:** who is responsible for whom, and what their roles are.

- **an overall description of the delivery process**, covering:
  - registration
  - inductions
  - assessment planning
  - assessment procedures
  - quality assurance procedures (internal and external verification)
  - certification

- **the IV process** (both formative and summative)

- **measures you will take to maintain and develop scheme delivery**, such as staff development, and how you will achieve this.

- **examples of the recording documentation you intend to use.** (These can be included in an annex and referred to.)

One centre's IV strategy

Here is an extract from one centre's verification strategy for introducing a new scheme to deliver learning and development qualifications at Levels 3 and 4. The strategy is written for assessors, verifiers and support staff – everyone involved in the administration, management or delivery of the full NVQs – and sets out procedures for assessing and verifying. (The centre has a separate IV strategy for delivering assessor and verifier awards.)

This is just one example of a strategy. There's no 'blueprint' for writing one, and your own strategies will vary from centre to centre, according to the schemes you offer and your organisation's staffing structures and resources.

Assessment

Assessment planning

1 All candidates undertaking learning and development awards must have an assessment plan for *every* assessment occasion. (This applies to both full qualifications and unit awards.)

2 The assessment-planning phase is vital. You need to ensure that the candidate knows what they are being assessed on, what methods will be used and what evidence they agree to provide.

3 Plans must be produced *before* assessment takes place.

4 Assessment planning should only be undertaken once the candidate is confident and competent in their job role, and after they have met any training or development needs.

Carrying out assessment

1 Assessment must be based on the candidate's work activities.

2 *Only* when they are working well in their roles, and are confident and competent in what they are doing, should you start to assess candidates' performance.

3 The majority of assessments should be via observation in the workplace, coupled with examination of work products, questioning/professional discussion and witness testimonies from relevant personnel.

4 You must record how you made your decision, the evidence you assessed and the methods you used.

5 You must ensure that all candidates produce evidence to meet the *entire* standard, as well as capturing the mandatory evidence requirements.

Independence of assessment (for full NVQs at Level 3 or 4)

For each candidate, another assessor from within the centre who meets the occupational competencies as defined in the L&D assessment strategy will act as assessor for a significant component of the candidate's NVQ. We will specify and review this at our initial team induction meeting once we have received approval for the scheme.

Internal verification

All internal verifiers must:

1 support their team of assessors by:
   - recording minutes of their meetings
   - carrying out assessor inductions
   - recording any advice given to assessors.

2 ensure the assessment and occupational competence of their assessors.
   - Observe assessors at least once a year for experienced assessors and every six months for inexperienced assessors.
   - Undertake formative verification of assessors' candidates and also conduct reviews with them on their progress.
   - Conduct standardisation meetings once every four months as well as regular team meetings, and keep all minutes of meetings in the centre file.
   - Contact their assessors at least once a month and record any conversations and action requirements.
   - Ensure that their centre is operating in accordance with the awarding body and NVQ Code of Practice regulatory requirements.
   - Contribute to external verification meetings.
   - Show that they are fully active in the quality assurance of their centre's provision.

Summative verification

All internal verifiers must undertake summative verification as follows:

1 All candidate portfolios should be sampled, including:
   - every unit that the independent assessor assesses
   - a further unit assessed by the primary assessor.

2 This sample will be allocated by the Eastwood Park centre and monitored by the Quality Assurance Co-ordinator.

3 The sampling strategy will be confirmed at our team induction meeting.

4 Feedback must be given to the assessor and relevant documentation kept within the centre.

Resources

Making sure you have sufficient resources is part of setting up effective assessment and verification. These resources will need to be in place before you can offer assessment to learners. Resourcing means having:

- physical resources – training rooms, documentation and equipment, for example – to enable you to deliver and evaluate the effectiveness of assessment within your centre.

- the right staffing structure for the numbers and types of learners you will be assessing.

Staffing

To work out staffing levels, you will need to calculate the realistic workload of each assessor and compare this with your anticipated number of learners.

Working out assessment capacity

Here's the procedure one senior verifier uses to work out her assessment capacity:

- Ask an experienced assessor to work out how long it takes them to assess a particular NVQ. Consider adding another half a day for new or inexperienced assessors, as they may need more time to begin with.

- Ask the new assessor to skill scan themselves against the A1 standards so that they gain a clear understanding of what they need to do.

- Talk to the assessor about the time it takes an experienced assessor to complete the NVQ. This should give the assessor an idea of what they need to do and how long it will take.

- Add in time for team meetings, standardisation meetings and CPD.

- Now ask the assessor to take account of their existing commitments against the time needed to deliver one NVQ. This should enable individual assessors to identify the number of learners they can realistically take on.

- Remember to allocate time on an individual basis, as each assessor will have different circumstances such as existing numbers of learners, training commitments or part-time hours.

- Build in things like sick leave, holidays and any CPD requirements, as set out within the assessment strategy (for example, assessors in hairdressing must spend 30 hours per year updating their practice within the salon).

You will also have to work out your verification capacity. If, as a result of your calculations, you discover that your capacity doesn't match actual or anticipated numbers of learners, you will need to adjust your staffing levels accordingly or cut down on the amount of registrations.

Here are some questions to answer when considering staffing structures and levels:

- Do you have enough assessors and, if so, can you justify their workload? (If you can't answer yes to this, you may need to work it out along the lines suggested above.)

- Are your assessors working to their maximum potential? For example, are they up to date with current assessment practices – particularly in carrying out 'holistic' assessments – and are they making best use of time? You may need to cast a critical eye over existing practice and be prepared to retrain if you are to answer these questions honestly.

- Similarly, have you worked out your verification capacity? For example, are your verifiers doing too much assessing? And if so, is this preventing them from operating to the full V1 standards?

- Have you taken administration staff into account? They also form part of the staffing structure and play a vital support role in providing you with management information, as well as helping you track learners' progress, process claims for certification and ensure confidentiality.

- What about your part-timers and/or subcontractors? They need to become an integral part of your QA process and this, in turn, may mean allowing more time for reviewing, assessment planning, talking to employers and attending meetings.

Remember...

Overloading assessors means compromising the integrity of the awards you offer. In England, Wales or Northern Ireland, if your assessors are found to have insufficient time, resources or authority to carry out their role, you risk losing your centre's direct claims status. This is a Level 2 sanction within the NVQ Code of Practice, and means that all claims for certification would need to be authorised by your external verifier.

Issues

Some of the managerial issues you may have to deal with are listed below, with suggestions for what you might do to resolve them.

Issue	Possible reasons	Suggestion
Verification is not a managerial role within your current staffing structure.	Senior managers may not know about the changes to verification and assessment practice or the NVQ Code of Practice and its implications.	Outline the main changes in the new standards to senior management. Explain the implications for future centre status if changes aren't made.
It isn't your job to... ...write quality assurance policies ... induct new assessors ... write job descriptions etc.	It is now. Changes to verification standards mean that the internal verifier is responsible for setting up and implementing quality-assurance procedures.	Make sure you have an input into your organisation's QA procedures. This may mean meeting with the quality team and/or senior managers and asking for verification policies and procedures to become a part of overall QA.
You have a lot of part-time assessors who aren't part of your 'core' team.	You or they may not see contributing to QA as part of their role.	*All* assessors need to contribute to the QA process. This means writing it into assessors' job descriptions and dealing with issues of payment and contractual obligations with any existing part-timers.

Managing communication

As the internal verifier, part of your role involves managing communication, both internally (with your own learners and team(s) of assessors) and externally (with the external verifier and the awarding body).

Here are some pointers to help you communicate effectively with all those involved in assessment and verification.

Managing communication is about...	This means...
Gaining the support of senior management and keeping them informed.	Formally reporting on any changes or modifications needed with regard to roles and responsibilities and centre practices and procedures, and the rationale for these.
Making sure that the assessment team and senior managers understand all your NVQ policies and procedures and their implications.	Setting out formal, documented QA procedures. Setting out a formal policy for internal verification, including reporting arrangements and your sampling strategy. Keeping a staff handbook and updating it regularly. Keeping minutes of team and standardisation meetings and circulating them to everyone involved.
Ensuring that everyone within your centre knows who does what and who is accountable to whom across all assessment sites.	Writing job descriptions. Keeping a clear record of roles, responsibilities and accountability. Drawing up an organisational chart for assessment and verification.
Ensuring that learners understand their right to access fair assessment policies and practices and what they can do if they have a query or a grievance.	Telling learners about your policies and procedures at induction. Making sure that the candidate can refer to a named person if necessary.
Keeping in touch with learners.	Making time to review with learners. Evaluating learner satisfaction. Devising an effective sampling strategy.
Maintaining effective communication with the awarding body.	Notifying them of any changes to your assessor and verifier teams and resources. Keeping records of all your communications with the awarding body.

Monitoring the QA process

Once you have quality-assurance policies and procedures in place, you need to monitor them to see whether or not they are working. This means using both qualitative and quantitative sources of data to give you a balanced picture.

Quantitative sources are where to look for 'hard' data such as facts and figures (like details of achievement rates and learners' start and finish dates). Qualitative sources will tell you what people think or feel about things; good examples are candidate surveys and feedback on internal verification reports.

For example, if your organisation's achievement rates took a dip, you would want to talk to assessors and learners to find out the reasons why (qualitative sources). In addition, you would monitor recruitment numbers and unit assessments (quantitative sources) to identify if particular schemes or qualifications were the source of the problem.

Here are some sources of information to use when monitoring your QA procedures. Most will give you both qualitative and quantitative data, as the examples show.

Information source	Example of qualitative information	Example of quantitative information
Assessor reports	The type of feedback given to learners	The number of assessment visits carried out over a period of time
Learner reviews	What learners say about their progress	The number of reviews carried out
Observations of assessment practice	How assessors behave with learners when assessing	The average number of observations required for each NVQ
Documentation used for tracking progress	The effectiveness of the system you use	Who has completed what unit and when
		The average length of time it takes a learner to complete the NVQ
Learners' evidence	The quality of training provision (by inference)	The take-up and use of a particular assessment method by assessors (such as professional discussion)
Employer surveys	What employers think of your training provision	The percentage of employers who reply

Self-check

The question-and-answer checklist below will help you identify where you are with regard to setting up and monitoring your QA procedures.

Question	Yes	No
Have we audited our current assessment and verification provision?	☐	☐
Do we have a QA system in place that meets the requirements of the NVQ Code of Practice?	☐	☐
Is there a formal, written internal verification policy for the organisation?	☐	☐
Is there a formal, written IV strategy specific to each scheme?	☐	☐
Do we have formal policies and procedures for:		
▪ equal opportunities?	☐	☐
▪ health and safety?	☐	☐
▪ appeals and grievances?	☐	☐
▪ bullying and harassment?	☐	☐
▪ data protection and candidate confidentiality?	☐	☐
Have we a realistic staffing structure in place?	☐	☐
Do we have sufficient resources?	☐	☐
Do we have formal communications procedures for:		
▪ learners?	☐	☐
▪ the assessment team?	☐	☐
▪ the verification team?	☐	☐
▪ senior managers?	☐	☐
▪ the external verifier?	☐	☐
▪ the awarding body?	☐	☐
Do we monitor our systems regularly?	☐	☐
Do all assessors and IVs undertake annual CPD and have plans that reflect the effectiveness of their professional development?	☐	☐
Do we use the information we gain from monitoring what we do to change what we do?	☐	☐

You are aiming to answer yes in all cases. Where you have answered no, you will need to take action.

Training and supporting assessors

This part of your role is about making sure you have the right people to carry out assessment and equipping them to do the job. It involves:

- identifying and agreeing criteria for choosing and supporting assessors within your organisation, and applying these

- supporting and developing your team

- managing the induction of assessors and producing supporting resources as necessary

- managing your team's performance through appraisal and your verification duties, including observing their assessment practice

- making sure ongoing CPD requirements are met, as required by each NVQ scheme's assessment strategy and within the NVQ Code of Practice.

What the standards say

Element V1.2   Support assessors

Verifiers need to:

- ensure that assessors have appropriate technical and vocational experience.

- ensure that assessors are familiar with and can carry out the specific assessment and follow the recording and internal audit procedures.

- identify the development needs of assessors in line with assessments, the needs of candidates and technical expertise and competence.

- give assessors the chance to develop their assessment experience and competence, and monitor their progress.

- ensure that assessors have regular opportunities to standardise assessment decisions

- monitor how assessors are capable of maintaining standards.

What assessors need to know and do

This section will help you think about the kind of person needed to carry out the assessor's job. You can select and adapt items from the following bullet lists and use them in job descriptions, person specifications and/or recruitment criteria.

Knowledge

Assessors need to know:

- the standards for which they are assessing

- the occupational area within which they are assessing

- how they fit into the overall delivery of the NVQ for which they will be assessing – who runs the training and when

- what the QA requirements are and how assessors must contribute

- what the NVQ Code of Practice and assessment strategy mean for the delivery and assessment of their NVQ

- how their CPD will contribute to quality improvement.

Competence

Assessors need to be able to:

- induct learners and explain the assessment process to them

- plan assessment and contribute to the learners' learning programmes

- assess using a variety of methods including accreditation of prior learning or achievement

- explain their assessment decisions and how they reached them

- give feedback to learners

- review progress

- keep records at each stage of the assessment process

- identify additional support requirements for their learners and ensure that these are met (for example, arranging access to special assessment requirements)

- make suggestions for improvements (contributing to the QA process)

- identify and address their own technical and vocational development needs.

Other qualities

The kind of person you might be seeking will depend to a large extent upon the type of organisation you are and the kind of learners you deal with. However, you may want to look for someone who possesses the following qualities:

- good written and face-to-face communication skills

- diplomacy and tact (when dealing with employers, for example)

- someone sympathetic to the needs of your learners

- good organisational skills such as the ability to plan their own workload

- a willingness to examine their own working practices and to seek improvements

- someone able to work both as part of a team and on their own (if part of the job involves travelling and visiting learners in their places of work, for example).

Identifying your centre's special requirements

Identify any additional criteria you want to add to the assessors' job specification for your centre. Remember to include particular requirements in relation to occupational competence or CPD, and special qualities that you feel your assessors need.

Make notes under each of the following headings:

Our assessors need to know:

Our assessors need to demonstrate:

Our assessors need the following:
Essential qualities:

Desirable qualities:

Remember...

Someone with the right occupational competence and experience may not necessarily make the best assessor. This is why it's so important to specify the qualities and attributes you want from your assessors to help you recruit the right kind of person at the start.

Supporting and developing assessors

Part of your job is to develop the competence of your team of assessors and to support them in their roles. In practice this means making sure of the following:

1 All your assessors keep up to date with current assessment practice.

For experienced assessors, this will mean that their existing practice meets the new A1 occupational standard. A good starting point is to get them to self-assess their current skills and activities against the A1 standards. You can then corroborate this by observing them in action. (ENTO's view is that all practising assessors and verifiers should aim to requalify to the new standards over time.)

Although there is no mandatory requirement to do so, you may want them to update their practice through achieving the A1 award for assessors or, even better, by achieving the Certificate in Review and Assessment of Learners. Section 4, 'Getting qualified' on page 69, gives more information on learning and development awards.

2 You and your assessors meet the continuing professional development requirements of your sectors.

All NVQs offered within different occupational areas have their own assessment strategies. These are constantly being revised, and you need to keep up to date with any changes via the relevant awarding bodies.

3 Assessors take ownership of their learning and development.

If you have new assessors, you may need to point them in the direction of the awarding body, their sector's Sector Skill Council (SSC) or other professional bodies in the first instance. In the long run, however, assessors need to demonstrate their commitment to CPD within their occupational area and to bring their individual training or development needs to your attention. They won't do this on their own; they will need your help and encouragement. See the checklists for assessors on pages 58 and 63. You may wish to adapt these for use with your own staff to establish a starting point.

It isn't only assessors who need to evaluate and develop their own practice. As a verifier, you too need to demonstrate that you have undertaken relevant professional development. See the checklists on pages 31 and 39.

4 New assessors are inducted into your organisation.

New members of your team will need time to familiarise themselves with your organisation and ways of working. To facilitate this process, you can:

- produce a handbook for assessors and another for internal verifiers, describing all procedures and documentation
- think of induction as happening over a period of time, rather than being just a day or a week-long event
- plan a variety of induction activities for assessors and verifiers, such as:
  - an information-giving event
  - work shadowing with an experienced assessor
  - a coaching session: observing the person assessing or verifying in action and offering training and support.

Make sure you fit in with existing arrangements for inducting new staff. You may request some time during your organisation's formal induction period, for example.

However you do it, be sure to keep records of your induction programme. Ask assessors to sign to say that they have received all the materials and understand their responsibilities, as this will show commitment to their role.

> *Remember...*
>
> *Although assessors and verifiers who hold the D units don't have to requalify to the A and V units, as the person responsible for staff development you should encourage your staff to visit the new standards and requalify eventually. This would be part of their continuing professional development (CPD).*

Training and development

The Teacher Development Co-ordinator at Loughborough College, Patsy Garner, describes the NVQ staffing structure and recent training and development at the college as follows:

'We don't have a central NVQ assessor and verifier department. Each curriculum team is responsible for its own NVQ delivery, assessment and verification, following college guidelines. Each team has a representative on the NVQ network group that we set up and developed over the past year. Last year the NVQ network group met twice a term. This year we are meeting once a term. We support each other and share good practice – at meetings a specific item on the agenda is set aside for "sharing good practice". We've also developed a part of the staff intranet where good practice is shared among all staff, and there's a specific NVQ area on our intranet. We've also had training on the new NVQ Code of Practice and its implications. As a result of this, we've updated our IV Guide to reflect the changes and developed a brand-new assessor guide.'

Managing your team's performance

As the person responsible for the quality of assessment, you need actively to manage the performance of your team. This means monitoring what they do as individuals and giving them feedback where necessary. There are two reasons for this:

- Monitoring performance is the way to ensure that assessment decisions are applied consistently, and is a fundamental part of the verification process (more about this on page 32, in 'Verifying the assessment process').

- Giving feedback on performance is part of developing and supporting your team. Appraising performance on a regular basis and giving positive and negative feedback will enable you and your assessors to pinpoint areas of good practice and areas for improvement. As a result, you will be able to formulate and agree development plans with each assessor.

Effective feedback

Any feedback you give assessors should follow the same principles as assessors giving feedback to learners on their performance. Here are some things to bear in mind:

- Don't just think about giving feedback – encourage your assessors to ask questions and to give you feedback too. Think of it as a two-way process, a partnership where you have a common goal of improving the overall quality of assessment.

- Remember to include positive feedback. Identifying and sharing areas of good practice is important and you should give credit where credit is due.

- Let your assessor take the lead in identifying possible areas for development. Here are some prompts you could use when it comes to identifying development needs. Ask them to tell you about:
  - their strengths and weaknesses when it comes to assessment (giving recent examples)
  - any areas or learners where they experience difficulties
  - anything they are particularly pleased about or they feel they have done especially well.

- Use any observations of performance as the basis for giving feedback. Stick to the facts – what you saw them do – particularly when delivering negative feedback.

- Keep records of all contacts with your assessors.

Here's how your log might look:

Assessor name	Date contacted	Reason for contact	Action agreed	Target date	Date achieved

Make sure that you maintain confidentiality when giving feedback to assessors on their performance. Don't give them oral feedback in front of learners, or let learners see or sign written observations or reports on performance management.

Internal verifiers *do* ask learners for feedback on their assessors' performance, but you need to treat this separately.

Self-check

The following question-and-answer checklist will help you identify possible areas for action when training and supporting your assessors.

Question	Yes	No	Not sure
Do all our assessors hold current assessor qualifications?	☐	☐	☐
If 'yes':			
■ Are all our assessors holding D units updating to the A1 standards?	☐	☐	☐
■ Are they operating to the new standards yet?	☐	☐	☐
■ Do all designate (trainee) assessors have action plans for completing their awards within 18 months?	☐	☐	☐
Do assessors meet the relevant assessment strategy requirements concerning their occupational competence?	☐	☐	☐
Do we encourage our assessors to evaluate and develop their own practice?	☐	☐	☐
Are assessors given regular feedback on their performance?	☐	☐	☐
Do assessors see any feedback they gain as a positive contribution to their CPD?	☐	☐	☐
Have we identified individual training needs, and does each assessor have a development plan?	☐	☐	☐
Have we taken account of changes to the assessment strategy in any plans to upskill our assessors and/or verifiers?	☐	☐	☐
Do we have recruitment criteria and job descriptions for assessors?	☐	☐	☐
Do we have a planned induction?	☐	☐	☐

You will need to take action in cases where you have ticked 'no' or 'not sure'.

Verifying the assessment process

Verifying is about standardising assessment decisions and processes. This means making sure that all assessors are assessing in similar ways to the required standards across all sites. The way to do this is to understand the basis on which assessors have made their assessment decisions, and to be confident that they are applying their judgements fairly and consistently, both with learners and when compared with other assessors.

This means:

- having a procedure for sampling the work of assessors and learners, and following it

- identifying problem areas and inconsistencies, and dealing with them

- standardising assessors' judgements and the quality of their documentation

- ensuring that the requirements of the awarding body and the appropriate assessment strategy are met, and submitting certification claims to the awarding body.

What the standards say

Element V1.3   Monitor the quality of assessors' performance

Verifiers need to:

- ensure that individual assessors are preparing for and planning assessments effectively.

- ensure that individual assessors have effective processes for making assessment decisions.

- ensure that individual assessors understand the necessary outcomes.

- ensure that individual assessors apply safe, fair, valid and reliable methods of assessing candidates' competence.

- check individual assessor's judgements to ensure they are consistent over time and with different candidates, including watching them carry out assessments.

- check a sufficient number of assessors to ensure consistency between assessors over time and with different candidates.

- check different assessment sites to ensure the consistency of assessment decisions.

- ensure that assessors set up and maintain effective working relationships with candidates at all stages of the assessment process.

- ensure assessors apply relevant health, safety and environmental protection procedures, as well as equality and access criteria.

- monitor how often assessment reviews take place and how effective these are.

- monitor how often assessors give feedback to candidates and how effective this is.

- monitor how accurate and secure assessors' record-keeping is.

- give assessors accurate and helpful feedback on their assessment decisions.

When should verification take place?

There are no hard and fast rules about when to carry out internal verification, but you may find it helpful to think in terms of formative and summative verification.

Formative (interim) verification

Formative verification describes your ongoing arrangements for sampling assessments and sharing good assessment practice. Think of formative assessment as 'dipping in and out of the assessment process' as you go along.

Formative methods include:

- observing your assessors assessing learners' competence
- reviewing with learners
- conducting team and standardisation meetings
- sampling evidence of performance that learners put forward, to ensure that assessors' judgements meet the standards.

Summative verification

This means carrying out objective checks on completed schemes, to ensure that the quality and integrity of the award have been maintained. Think of summative verification as 'summing up'.

You should carry out summative assessment by sampling the work of assessors and learners when particular schemes or units have been completed.

Sampling

You need a formal sampling strategy for each NVQ scheme; sampling isn't something you can do as and when you feel like it. Here are some areas to include in your plans:

Observing assessors' performance
You will need to vary the size of your sample and rate at which you sample, to take account of:

- the amount of experience the assessor has (a new assessor would need to be observed more often and with a larger number of candidates, for example)
- the introduction of a new scheme
- problems or difficulties with particular units.

Use of different assessment methods and how decisions are reached
Here you should aim to sample all of the following:

- assessors
- units
- assessment sites
- candidate cohorts.

Reviewing assessment with learners

Here's what verifiers say about using reviews to verify assessment practice:

'I make it my business to know what's going on with learners. I just carry out a normal review with them, but I've got questions in my mind about the way they've been assessed that I want answers to – and I make sure I get them.'

'Our candidates know we come round and review and why. We see it as part of our quality procedures and our appeals process and we tell them what's going to happen and when at induction.'

'When I compared our reviews with progress and achievement documentation I could see we were wasting time. What we needed to do was to carry out more assessment visits later on, when learners were producing good evidence to the standards. We needed to work smarter – not just visit learners because we had to, but plan exactly what we were doing and why. We're still in the process of planning this but we're definitely going to be more flexible about timings in future because we'll know where each learner is and exactly what we want to achieve.'

Here are some further points to consider:

- Build in time to analyse the information you gain as a result of sampling, and to reflect on what this means for assessment practice generally.

- Make sure that, overall, your sampling strategy covers all the units of the qualification, all assessors, all locations, all candidates and all assessment methods.

- Ensure that records are produced for all types of verification and that they contain both quantitative and qualitative data.

- Make sure your systems and procedures – standardisation meetings, sampling procedures, reviews and the like – work for you. Be prepared to use the information you gain as a result of verification to change anything that isn't helping.

As you sample, keep a written rationale of what you do and why. (This should be clearly communicated in your IV strategy.) In this way, you can justify any decisions you make to the awarding body, or as a result of appeals. You will also have a record to form the basis of any reports you need to write for your external verifier or your manager.

Increase the size of your sample and sample more frequently if you have introduced a new assessment scheme or changed your assessment practice.

Explain what you intend to do for each NVQ scheme and make this part of your internal verification strategy. Do this by listing the steps you will take, and when.

Ultimately, you are making sure that assessors have assessed their learners in the right way, using the best methods, and have recorded their judgements to provide an 'audit trail' so that everyone can see the basis on which decisions about learners' competence have been made.

'When observing assessors, I don't go for forms or tick boxes. I write down the main points about what I see in the order in which it happens, then I take it from there.' Internal verifier

'When I started observing assessors over a period of time, I realised that we were driven primarily by the evidence requirements of the various NVQs, because what the assessors did was go straight to this when planning assessments and evidence collection. This led to a piecemeal approach – and huge portfolios.' Internal verifier

Remember...

As the verifier, you aren't assessing learners' evidence – your assessors do this. You're verifying assessors' judgements to ensure that they meet the requirements of the appropriate assessment strategies. Since you're also ensuring that assessors apply judgements consistently, you're comparing and sharing good practice too.

Assessment methods

Here are some things to look out for when verifying assessment methods. Your awarding body will have specific guidance on the different methods to use, and you should follow this when carrying out verification.

Method	Things to look for
Observations of performance	This is a primary source of evidence, so check that there is enough to meet the standards in question.
	Observations of performance are normally backed up by questioning or professional discussion to cover knowledge requirements or 'gaps' where the assessor is unable to observe the learner in action, or where performance is implicit in what the learner is doing.
Witness testimony (use of another's contribution)	Agree on how assessors will report the use of another's contribution to you, and under what circumstances.
	You aren't necessarily looking for a signed checklist here. Evidence that the assessor has talked to the person in question is acceptable. You may want this to be recorded in some way and, if so, will want your assessor to indicate the key points covered and how these relate to the standards.
Questioning	Check that all your assessors are using questioning in similar ways.
	Don't use prepared lists.
	Ensure that questions are only relevant to the learner's performance in their workplace.
Simulation	Check that simulation is allowed, by looking at the relevant assessment strategy. If it is, make sure that it is not used on its own or as a primary source of evidence.
	Ensure that assessors have sought approval from you first, before undertaking any form of simulation.
Examination of work products	Make sure that you standardise the use of work products with your assessors. Specify and agree examples of what to look for, the extent to which they can be used and for which standards, and the amount of evidence needed. These need to be authentic, relevant to the standards and directly relevant to the learner's work.
	Where learners have put forward a substantial work activity covering several units (such as a project or assignment), you will need to check that these have been assessed holistically, that is, using an appropriate mix of assessment methods over time.
Use of videos and/or audio cassettes	These are fine to use as a means of recording performance or in the absence of a 'live' performance for the assessor, as long as all parties give their approval and are comfortable with the medium.
	Be sensitive to issues of confidentiality or security (again, ensure that appropriate permissions have been obtained).
	Look for annotations and references to sections of the tape and descriptions of highlights from the assessor, as this shows you that they have assessed the key points.
	Standardise occasions when you would use tapes and videos of performance, and agree areas of performance you would like to see highlighted.
Professional discussion	Here, you are looking for a tape and/or a report outlining the key points of the discussion and how they link to the standards.
	Again, standardise occasions when professional discussion is to be used with assessors, and agree areas of performance you would like to see highlighted.

Identifying inconsistencies

Here are some questions to ask when verifying assessment:

- Was this assessment planned in detail with the learner so as to maximise his or her chances of success?

- Has the assessor made a judgement based on enough evidence to meet the standards – particularly given the range of contexts or conditions specified?

- Has the assessor made best use of the assessment methods available?

- Has the assessor used the right assessment methods, as laid down in the appropriate assessment strategy?

- Does the way in which the evidence has been presented make it easy to find and understand?

- Can I be sure that the evidence has been produced by the learner, and only by him or her?

- Overall, is this is a 'safe' judgement on the assessor's part?

- Have I and the assessor used 'VACS' to ensure that the evidence is:
  - **valid**   appropriate to the standards
  - **authentic** the candidate's own work
  - **current**   still applicable to the standards
  - **sufficient** enough to demonstrate competence over time?

You should aim to answer yes to all the above questions. If you answer no to any of them, this will alert you to possible areas of inconsistency and the need for further action on your part.

Sharing good practice

To standardise assessment practice among your assessors, you'll need to get together to discuss and agree how assessment decisions are made. This means holding meetings regularly across your centre(s).

- **Standardisation meetings** are specific to each scheme you offer, and where you and your assessors look at specific elements or units within the scheme to identify the evidence produced by the candidates and examine the assessment methods used. This enables you to:
  - determine the types and amounts of evidence you expect learners to produce to meet the standards in question
  - decide the best methods to use when assessing these standards
  - ensure that all assessors have similar expectations and are assessing with the same rigour across all learners.

- **Team meetings** cover more general issues, and may involve all those concerned with the delivery of your scheme, such as trainers or administration staff as well as assessors. At team meetings you may cover issues affecting the delivery of all NVQs or awards, such as centre procedures or record keeping.

As the internal verifier, it's your job to call both team and standardisation meetings and to chair them. This means:

- setting a date, a time and an agenda

- making sure that detailed minutes are produced and circulated

- feeding back the results of any sampling you have done

- passing on to assessors information from the external verifier or awarding body concerning assessment practices and procedures

- having the final say in decisions about assessment practice and procedures.

'We had one inexperienced assessor who was inconsistent in comparison to everyone else. I realised that meetings weren't enough, so I arranged for her to shadow a more experienced assessor to get the idea, then I increased my sampling rate. It was worth it in the long run, as I was able to give her feedback on how she was improving.'

Internal verifier

Standardising practice

Here are some of the things assessors and verifiers do when standardising practice:

'We bring in our learners' portfolios and swap them around.'

'We look at the standards and agree the areas that are causing us the most difficulties, then discuss how we are going to assess them.'

'We get lots of candidates with special needs – particularly those with English as a second language – so we have to be very careful to treat all candidates the same across the different schemes we offer. We hold special meetings with assessors to discuss this across our training centres just to make sure we're all doing the same things with learners.'

'Our internal verifier sets the agenda for our meetings, usually as a result of her visits or sampling. Then it's over to us. We agree how to tackle each item as a team and get our IV to confirm the definitive answer.'

'We're part of an NHS Trust so our hospital is one half of a dozen or so satellite centres. I'm the internal verifier for all the care NVQs within our hospital. We hold monthly team meetings within our centre and standardisation meetings at the Trust's premises three or four times a year.'

The NVQ Code of Practice

The practices and procedures you have met in this section are requirements for all centres and are set out in the NVQ Code of Practice. If you embrace the concept of assuring quality, you are unlikely to encounter problems with measuring your performance against the criteria it contains and setting targets for improvement as necessary.

Non-compliance in certain aspects of verification leads to sanctions, as shown below.

Example of non-compliance   **Sanction**

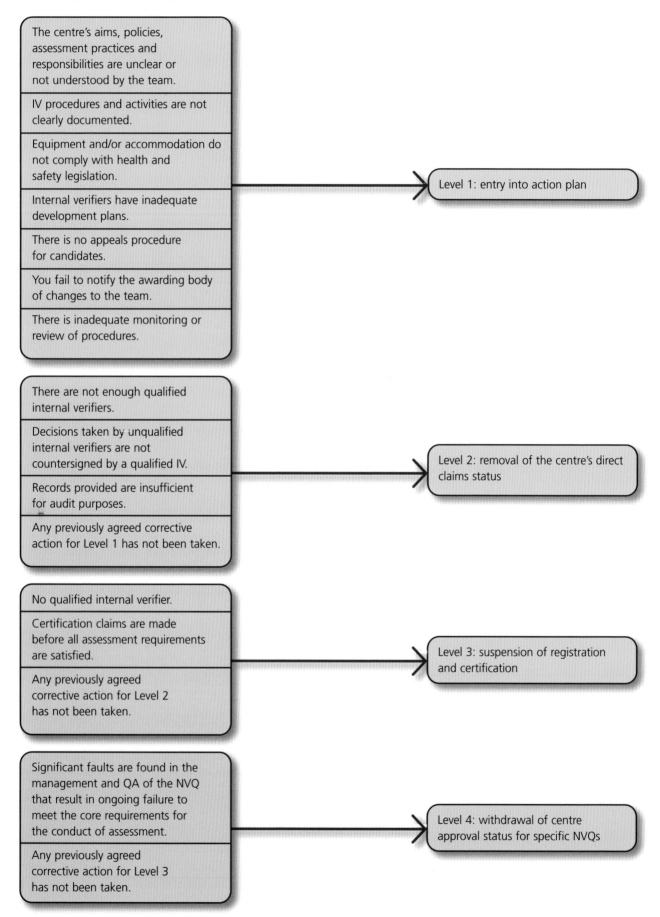

The centre's aims, policies, assessment practices and responsibilities are unclear or not understood by the team.

IV procedures and activities are not clearly documented.

Equipment and/or accommodation do not comply with health and safety legislation.

Internal verifiers have inadequate development plans.

There is no appeals procedure for candidates.

You fail to notify the awarding body of changes to the team.

There is inadequate monitoring or review of procedures.

Level 1: entry into action plan

There are not enough qualified internal verifiers.

Decisions taken by unqualified internal verifiers are not countersigned by a qualified IV.

Records provided are insufficient for audit purposes.

Any previously agreed corrective action for Level 1 has not been taken.

Level 2: removal of the centre's direct claims status

No qualified internal verifier.

Certification claims are made before all assessment requirements are satisfied.

Any previously agreed corrective action for Level 2 has not been taken.

Level 3: suspension of registration and certification

Significant faults are found in the management and QA of the NVQ that result in ongoing failure to meet the core requirements for the conduct of assessment.

Any previously agreed corrective action for Level 3 has not been taken.

Level 4: withdrawal of centre approval status for specific NVQs

Self-check

The following question-and-answer checklist will help you identify where you are with regard to effective verification.

Question	Yes	No
Do we have a formal IV strategy for each scheme?	☐	☐
Do we have formal sampling procedure and strategy?	☐	☐
Are all assessors allocated a named internal verifier who is responsible for them?	☐	☐
Are assessors observed in action?	☐	☐
Do internal verifiers include learners in the verification process?	☐	☐
Is the information gained as a result of verification fed back to assessors and acted upon?	☐	☐
Do we make a point of sharing good practice?	☐	☐
Do we hold regular standardisation meetings?	☐	☐
Do we hold regular team meetings for assessors and verifiers within each occupational area for which we offer NVQs?	☐	☐

You are aiming to answer yes in all cases. Where you have answered no, you will need to take action.

2 Assessment: part of the learning process

As an assessor, you play an important part in enabling learners to achieve their learning targets, by assessing their performance and giving them feedback on how well they are doing. You also ensure that national standards of competence are met and maintained. The key to effective assessment lies in your ability to make safe and reliable judgements.

This section concentrates on the assessor's main areas of responsibility, namely:

- *using assessment to plan learning*

- *using different assessment methods*

- *reaching and reporting your judgements*

- *giving learners feedback on their performance, and planning what happens next*

- *contributing to the centre's QA processes.*

Assessment should not take place in isolation from the learning process, but be planned to happen in an integrated way. It should only take place when your learners are ready.

Using assessment to plan learning

It is important to assess only when you are confident that the learner is performing to the standards. Assessors have input at key stages of learners' programmes, as follows:

Key stage   **The assessor...**

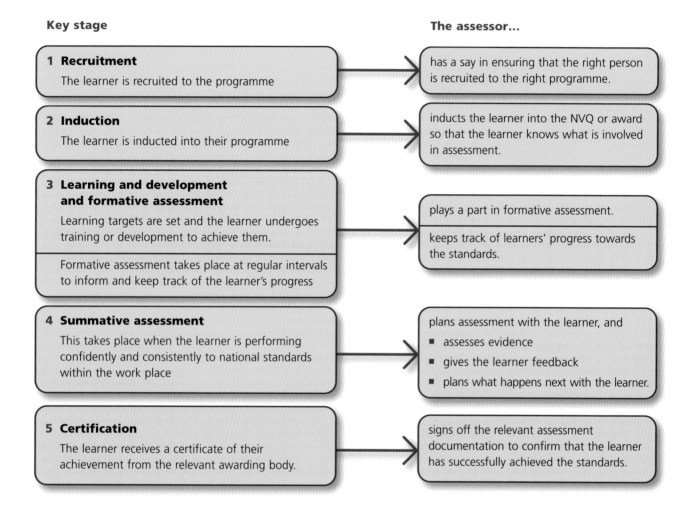

1 Recruitment
The learner is recruited to the programme

has a say in ensuring that the right person is recruited to the right programme.

2 Induction
The learner is inducted into their programme

inducts the learner into the NVQ or award so that the learner knows what is involved in assessment.

3 Learning and development and formative assessment
Learning targets are set and the learner undergoes training or development to achieve them.

Formative assessment takes place at regular intervals to inform and keep track of the learner's progress

plays a part in formative assessment.

keeps track of learners' progress towards the standards.

4 Summative assessment
This takes place when the learner is performing confidently and consistently to national standards within the work place

plans assessment with the learner, and
- assesses evidence
- gives the learner feedback
- plans what happens next with the learner.

5 Certification
The learner receives a certificate of their achievement from the relevant awarding body.

signs off the relevant assessment documentation to confirm that the learner has successfully achieved the standards.

What the standards say

Element A1.1   Develop plans for assessing competence with learners

Assessors need to:

- develop and agree an assessment plan with candidates.
- check that all candidates understand the assessment process and what is involved, the support available to them and the complaints and appeals procedure.
- agree fair, safe, valid and reliable assessment methods.
- identify appropriate and cost-effective opportunities for assessing performance.
- plan for using different types of evidence.
- identify how the past experiences and achievements of candidates will contribute to the assessment process.
- identify and agree any special arrangements needed to make sure the assessment process is fair.

- identify how other people will contribute to assessments and what support they may need.
- identify how to protect confidentiality and agree arrangements to deal with sensitive issues.
- agree how you will handle any difficulties or disputes during the assessment.
- agree when assessment will take place with candidates and the other people involved.
- agree arrangements with candidates for reviewing their progress against the assessment plan.
- review and update assessment plans to take account of what the candidates have achieved.

Formative and summative assessment

You can use assessment in two ways:

- **Formative assessment** is a means of informing the learning process, helping learners to see how well they are doing and adjusting learning targets and ways of achieving them as a result. Formative assessment methods include:

  - self-assessment checklists

  - reviews

  - peer assessments

  - discussions.

  Formative assessment methods are not normally used as proof of learners' ultimate levels of competence (you wouldn't include them in their portfolios, for example), but to record their progress towards achieving the standards.

- **Summative assessment** is usually introduced when formative assessment has done its job and the learner is ready to have their performance assessed ('summed up') against the standards they hope to achieve. Summative assessment methods include:

  - observing learners perform in the workplace

  - asking learners questions and finding out why they did things, through professional discussion or reflective accounts

  - examining work products produced by the candidate as part of their normal work

  - taking account of past experiences and achievements

  - using evidence from other people, including peers and witnesses

  - setting tests (if required by the appropriate assessment strategy)

  - setting projects and tasks (if you can't get access to natural performance evidence in the learner's workplace)

  - arranging simulations (again, if the scheme assessment strategy allows for this).

Formative and summative assessment work together. To be effective, summative assessment needs to take place when the learner is ready, in other words when they are consistently operating to the required standard in their workplace. You will only know when they have reached this point as a result of formative assessment.

You may not be responsible for assessing at each stage of the learning process as described above. An adviser or trainer might be responsible for initial and formative assessments. However, only you, the NVQ assessor, can carry out summative assessment.

'All our assessors are responsible for reviewing and tracking performance with learners. We have placement officers who carry out three-monthly reviews with each individual at their place of work, but they liaise with employers and assessors. If the learner has just had an assessment visit, the assessor may want to attend the progress review and discuss the results with all concerned.'
Internal verifier

Planning assessment with learners: your first meeting

The first phase of the assessment planning process happens right at the beginning, when the learner is recruited to a particular learning programme. At this stage your job is to help them gain an overview of the qualification they are hoping to achieve and to plan their route to achieving it – by selecting the right units, for example.

Ideally, all assessors should play a part in recruiting the right learner to the right programme. If you don't, you risk setting the learner up for disappointment or failure. (Most learners will vote with their feet and leave if they cannot succeed.)

You will find the following steps useful when planning assessment with learners in the early stages:

- Make sure you have an overview of all the relevant core and optional units within the learner's chosen qualification or scheme.

- Identify what the learner does on a day-to-day basis within their workplace, listing their main functions and responsibilities, then try and group these into key activities.

- Now link the units in the qualification to the key activities.

- You will usually find that any specialist activities that the learner carries out are linked to optional units.

- Focus on these optional units first. Usually, you will find that mandatory units contain generic competencies that underpin most of what the learner does and will probably occur naturally from carrying out the activities linked to the optional units.

- Once you have identified how the learner's work patterns fit in with the NVQ along with the most appropriate optional units, make sure that the learner has a list of all their allocated units.

Here are some further pointers to help you get the most out of your first meeting with the learner:

- Take account of the results of initial assessment. Make sure you have all the necessary documents to hand concerning the learner's existing achievements and their potential.

- Gauge the NVQ level at which the learner is currently working. Don't be put off if they are expecting to take the qualification at a different level. Explain that they won't be able to demonstrate their competence under the right conditions.

- Decide whether or not the learner's job and their aptitudes and attainments indicate that they are likely to succeed. If they don't, you should recommend that the learner not be recruited to the programme.

- If they do, find out if the learner has any particular assessment requirements (such as working shifts or part-time hours, which may mean making special arrangements).

Record the results of your meeting, and use these as part of your organisation's recruitment process and analysis of your training and assessment provision generally.

Planning assessment with learners: in-depth planning

Phase two of assessment planning involves more in-depth planning. With your learner, choose one or more of the key activities you identified during phase one, and focus on the optional unit(s) that are applicable. Now make the links with appropriate mandatory units.

Make decisions about each of the following and record them on an assessment plan:

- the activity the learner will be doing in the workplace

- the date, time and location of this activity

- the evidence he or she will be showing you

- the units or elements being covered by this assessment

- the most effective assessment methods for the activity and any related evidence.

Arrange a review date to follow this assessment, to tidy up loose ends and to plan for the next phase of assessment. Carry on planning in this way, by identifying the relevant optional units and gradually covering the mandatory units, until the learner has achieved his or her chosen award.

'I had a group of Early Years learners and their employer wanted them to take a Level 3 NVQ. It soon became clear that they wouldn't be able to achieve the standards as their job involved working under supervision – they weren't allowed to work with the children on their own. To get the Level 3 qualification you need to be in charge and you need to have the authority to make decisions.' Early years assessor

Remember...

Make sure that your plans are realistic and cost effective for the learner. This means:

- *choosing the best assessment method for the circumstances*

- *making the most of your assessment visits by identifying assessment opportunities well in advance, for example, and confirming these with the learner*

- *assessing 'holistically' (using a variety of methods and evidence to cover different units) and making the most of every assessment opportunity*

- *only assessing when the learner is ready (you will waste their time as well as yours if you don't)*

- *taking as your starting point for assessment and evidence gathering the main, naturally occurring activities they carry out within the workplace – not the standards.*

Don't be tempted to plan by following the order in which the standards are laid out – 'doing' the core units first followed by the optional units, for example. The NVQ will bear no resemblance to the learner's normal working patterns, and this can be demotivating for them.

Don't leave the optional units until the end. These are linked to the learner's 'specialisms', usually the most important part of their work.

Using different assessment methods

As an assessor, you need confidence in your own ability to reach a good assessment decision. The key to making a safe and reliable assessment judgement is to use the most appropriate method for the evidence with which you are presented and for the learner's needs and circumstances. You can be flexible and creative in your choice of method, *but* you must be able to justify its use and any subsequent decision you make.

This section contains information on the main assessment methods used by assessors and help with when to use them. Your awarding body will have specific guidance on the assessment methods to use in different schemes, so you will also need to find out this information.

What the standards say

Element A1.2 Judge evidence against criteria to make assessment decisions

Assessors need to:

- use the agreed assessment methods to assess competence in appropriate situations.

- use the past experiences and achievements of candidates as part of the assessment of their current competence.

- ensure that the evidence comes from the candidates' own work.

- make safe, fair, valid and reliable decisions about the competence of candidates, only on the agreed standard.

- collect evidence from the other people involved in the assessment process.

- apply any agreed special arrangements to make sure the assessment is fair.

- base your decisions on all the relevant evidence of candidates' performance and knowledge. Take this evidence from as many places as possible.

- explain and resolve any inconsistencies in the evidence.

- make a record of the outcomes of assessments by using the agreed recording system.

- speak to the appropriate person if you and the candidate cannot agree on your assessment of their performance.

Observation

You might argue that the most appropriate way of assessing learners' competence is to observe them in action, and you'd be right. Observation is the main method to use when assessing work-based competence. Most awarding bodies specify observation as a *primary* or *mandatory* method for assessing competence within their assessment schemes.

When observing, your job as the assessor is to:

- record or capture what you see
- ensure that the learner has the knowledge to back up what you see them do and that they can justify their competence
- identify achievements against the standards you are assessing
- ensure that the learner agrees with your decision – if not, instigate the appeals procedure. (This is why it is important for assessors and candidates to sign and date all records.)

If you are confident that observation has produced sufficient evidence, you can award the standards in question.

Here are some do's and don'ts to bear in mind when using observation:

Do	Don't
Think in terms of producing written records. These are more powerful for observations as you can use them more than once to cover other standards.	Rely solely on one observation as proof of the learner's ability to perform consistently and under different conditions. Back it up where necessary by using questioning to capture any knowledge that is inferred through performance.
Think in terms of producing a 'narrative' which describes the main points of what you see when recording your observations. (See the Assessor's report on page 54 for an example of how to do this.)	Assess without first planning and agreeing it with the learner (but take account of any naturally occurring evidence as it happens)
Ensure that all relevant people such as the learner and his or her employer know that the observation is taking place.	Be obtrusive – you'll put the learner off.
Use a Dictaphone or similar. These are great for capturing professional discussion and questioning.	Fill in pre-prepared checklists – they can be limiting. Use the standards as your main reference point instead.

Remember...

You will need to agree the best time for observations to take place with your learner. Involve the learner's employer or manager if you plan to observe the learner at a busy time, or when carrying out a sensitive task.

'People always talk about Christmas being the busiest time in retailing. It isn't a good time to release people for training but it's a brilliant time to observe because there's so much going on. It's important to see how learners perform under these conditions.'

Retail assessor

Questioning

Asking the learner questions follows observation naturally, and is the main method to use to find out whether or not your learner has the necessary underpinning knowledge and understanding of the tasks they are performing.

When questioning, you may need to find out more about the learner's implicit performance – something you may not have seen in action but which is an obvious part of the task or job. You may also want to question the learner about other aspects of their job that are related to the standards, such as what they might do under different circumstances or conditions.

Only give learners prepared questions in cases where you know the evidence is necessary (if you won't see them face to face, for example). Don't use prepared lists that are given out to all learners irrespective of their circumstances.

Don't ask leading questions, or you will find yourself making the wrong assumptions, or judging your own competence and not the learner's!

Here are some examples of different questioning techniques you can use and suggestions for when to use them.

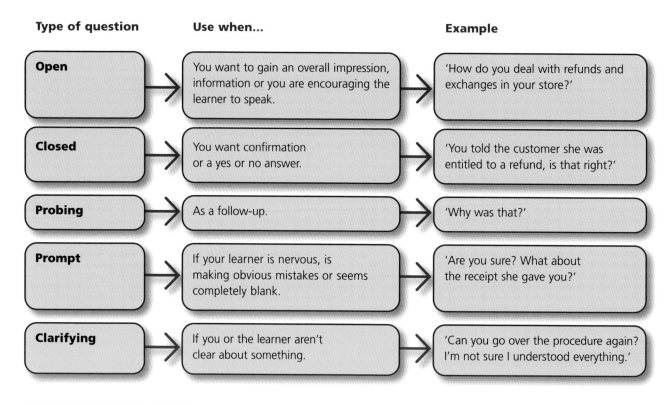

Type of question	Use when...	Example
Open	You want to gain an overall impression, information or you are encouraging the learner to speak.	'How do you deal with refunds and exchanges in your store?'
Closed	You want confirmation or a yes or no answer.	'You told the customer she was entitled to a refund, is that right?'
Probing	As a follow-up.	'Why was that?'
Prompt	If your learner is nervous, is making obvious mistakes or seems completely blank.	'Are you sure? What about the receipt she gave you?'
Clarifying	If you or the learner aren't clear about something.	'Can you go over the procedure again? I'm not sure I understood everything.'

Remember...

- *Only question learners on what is required in the standards, and nothing more.*
- *Try and link your questions directly to what the learner does and their competence within their workplace.*

Examination of work products

Work products are the outcomes of tasks that learners carry out as a result of the work they do. Products can be assessed as evidence of learners' competence, provided they meet the standards in question and have been produced as a result of real work.

You need to look at the standards and their associated assessment strategy for guidance on the types and amount of work products to look for.

Using projects and assignments

You can use a project or assignment:

- if circumstances mean the learner's normal performance is not accessible in the workplace

- if the project has been set up in their workplace as part of their job (such as a learner aiming for a management NVQ doing a project on health and safety for the benefit of the organisation).

However, before you assess the outcomes you need to be clear about why the learner has carried out a particular project or assignment. Often, projects are given to learners as part of their training and development – to gain experience or to practise under working conditions – in which case the outcomes do not provide real evidence of competence.

Learners need to be able to explain how their work products meet the standards. You can use questioning or professional discussion as additional assessment methods here. The same criteria apply when assessing the outcomes of projects or assignments.

Professional discussions

Professional discussions will enable you to gain a rounded picture of your learner's total performance. As an assessment method, it is one of the best ways to test the validity and reliability of the person's evidence, particularly if they have used a range of work-based activities covering a number of units. When used correctly, it also avoids the need for large portfolios and bureaucracy, as you can simply talk to your learner about their performance and the reasons behind their actions and decisions.

Here is a summary of what professional discussion is and isn't about:

Professional discussion is about ...	Professional discussion is *not* about ...
Planning with your candidate in advance the areas of the standards that will be under discussion and allowing your candidate to prepare for the discussion.	Using a pre-determined list of questions in a structured or mechanistic way.
Talking with the candidate about what he or she is doing and the reasons why – you are looking for evidence of decision-making and analytical abilities as well as proof of specific knowledge.	Having a friendly chat.
A gradual 'handing over' to the candidate. You would expect him or her to be taking the lead in any discussion after an initial session.	Written case studies, storyboards or photocopies of evidence.
Recording the main points of what the candidate says and how this relates to the relevant standards (using a bullet list, for example, supported by a tape recording of the discussion).	Recording verbatim what your learner says.
You acquiring skills in: - using video or audio equipment (discussions can be taped as long as you check first that the learner is comfortable with this) - managing the discussion process (moving your learner on, summarising, questioning and clarifying, for example) - picking out the key elements from the standards for which you are assessing, and concentrating on these.	You telling your learner what to do.

Witness testimony

A useful method of assessment to back up your observations of learners in action is the witness testimony. The person who supervises a learner's work performance on a regular basis, for example, is often in the best position to say whether or not the learner is performing consistently to the standards over time. Using this person's contribution (a 'witness testimony') confirms to you that the learner is competent in a particular area.

Here are some pointers for using a witness testimony. As the assessor, you need to ask:

- Does this person know what's being asked of them? (Have you or the learner briefed them?)

- Is this person's contribution *relevant* to both the standards and to the learner?

- Can he or she *verify the learner's competence* in the areas in question?

- Has he or she said *enough* to confirm the learner's competence?

- Is it a *recent* contribution?

Aim to answer yes in each case. Again, you can use a witness testimony in a variety of ways. As the assessor, you can ask for one or more of the following:

- A written report or narrative.

- A discussion with the person. This could be done either face to face, or by telephone or email.

If another's contribution is to be of any use as a witness testimony when it comes to assessment, your learner needs to know how to manage it. This means advising your learner to:

- brief the person in advance – supervisors and managers are usually busy

- explain the standards to be covered and provide the person with a copy of these, if necessary

- be specific about what the person needs to contribute. This might be:

  - describing occasions when they have seen the learner perform to the standards in question and the conditions under which they performed

  - adding notes to a project that the learner has carried out, and/or speaking to you, the assessor, about these.

Make sure the person signs and dates their contribution.

Simulation

You must make sure that simulations are allowed before using them as a method of assessment. Since competence-based assessment is generally about the learner's ability to perform under working conditions, the only occasions when simulations can be used are usually those involving issues of cost, privacy, confidentiality or safety. The standard-setting body for the sector will determine in their assessment strategy where simulation can be used. Before using any form of simulation, you should:

- check the assessment strategy to see if simulation is permitted

- seek confirmation from your internal verifier before you use it.

Assessing prior achievement

Part of your job is to assess what the learner brings with them in the way of existing achievements or learning and to gauge whether or not these constitute valid evidence of their performance towards the standards they are aiming for. This process is known as assessment of prior achievement (APA) or assessment of prior learning (APL).

The results of APA/APL should inform the learner's learning and development programme. This may not necessarily affect assessment, but will affect the type and amount of training needed. For example, if a learner has had a Saturday job within retailing, he or she may not be performing to the standards but will probably be able to show that they have gained the basics.

The process of APA – judging the evidence that your learner already brings with them – is the same as that for assessing all evidence. It should therefore be:

- valid

- authentic

- current

- sufficient.

The judgement you need to make is: does it meet the standards in question?

Reaching a judgement

By using an appropriate range of assessment methods, you should be in a position to make judgements about the learner's competence against the standards.

Ask the following questions:

Is the evidence ...

- **valid?** Does it meet the elements, performance criteria, range and/or knowledge requirements of the standards?

- **authentic?** Has the learner produced the evidence?

- **current?** Has it been produced recently and is the learner still able to demonstrate competence?

- **sufficient?** Is there enough evidence to prove that the learner has demonstrated competence over time and in a range of contexts?

For the learner to meet the standards in question, you must be able to answer yes confidently in each case and demonstrate to your internal verifier that you have undertaken this process against all the evidence your learner presents to you. (This is why it is important to get learners to date and sign all their evidence and your records.)

If you answer no to one or more of the above, this tells you that the learner is not yet competent.

Troubleshooting

Here are some examples of the issues you will have to deal with when reaching a sound judgement. The first two describe problems to do with authenticity of evidence and the third shows how the assessor dealt with evidence that was not current.

'I was assessing IT standards for a range of candidates and found some project evidence that was exactly the same in three of the portfolios. They had obviously copied each other's work and just printed it off! It helps to look under "Properties" on their files – sometimes we assessors have to be a bit of a sleuth!'

'One witness blatantly told a lie and said that his learner had operated a particular type of machinery on a regular basis, when I knew for a fact that his company did not possess such equipment. On questioning the witness, he said he thought it wasn't important and that he was doing his candidate a favour.'

'I recently had somebody who wanted to submit evidence for the APA process against achieving unit G3. They wanted to use the fact that they had achieved E31 from the TDLB standards six years ago. Obviously this was not current, so I checked to see if they were still evaluating their performance on a regular basis, and they had done nothing since achieving their award. This award and evidence was therefore not allowed.'

Don't be afraid to say no to evidence that you feel is unreliable; it's your job to do so.

Reporting your judgements

You need to report back formally on the judgements you have made as part of your centre's internal verification and quality procedures. This allows everyone to keep track of learners' achievement and provides a written record of all assessment decisions. Reports are important for the following reasons:

- for confirming to the learner what they have achieved

- for auditing and quality-assurance purposes

- to provide you with a written record in cases where your appeals procedure is invoked.

Your reports should contain the following:

- details of your learner, and the date, time and place of assessment. You also need to indicate the length of your assessment visit

- the evidence presented to you and the assessment methods you used

- cross-referencing to the standards in question

- your judgements

- any relevant action agreed

- dates and signatures from both you (the assessor) and your candidate.

On the following page is an assessor's report on an assessment visit with her candidate assessor. It shows a wide variety of assessment methods and the assessment decisions she made as a result.

Note that this assessor cannot confirm the candidate assessor's competence in one area of the standards because the candidate doesn't demonstrate knowledge of the appeals process. Have a look at the way in which the assessor handles this in her feedback to the candidate assessor so as to maintain their confidence.

Assessor report

Candidate's name: SC (candidate assessor)

Name of award: Certificate in review and assessment of learning

Assessor's name: BH

Location of assessment: Swinton Training Centre

Date of assessment: February 2004

Units/Elements assessed: A1, L16

Details of assessed activities	Unit/ element	PCs, range and knowledge achieved	Assessment methods
08:45: I meet SC and go through the planned assessment with her. She confirms that she is happy with the arrangements and is fully prepared.	A1.1	a,b,c,d,e,f,h,k,l,m	
09:00: SC greets her candidate, CH, introduces me and explains my role. She attempts to calm C's nerves.	A1.2		
S then shows me C's assessment plan. This contains the date of assessment, work-based activities, evidence to be provided by the candidate and appropriate assessment methods. She also shows me the candidate's portfolio containing previous assessments so that I can see the background and context for this assessment.	A 1.3	a,b,c,d,e,g,i a,b,c,f	Inspection of work products
Using professional discussion, S explains the reasons for her choice of assessment methods. She has used verbal and written evidence from C's centre manager as a witness for previous evidence she was unable to observe herself; observation to cover performance across the award; questions to cover gaps in evidence and to clarify knowledge; and professional discussion for her candidate to reflect on practice. She also explains that APA is to be used as evidence from her candidate's Level 1 award, along with a Health and Safety certificate.	A1.4	a	Professional discussion
09:35: I observe S speaking to C's line manager. She is using him as a witness to confirm C's competence concerning reporting procedures. She is using a Dictaphone, appropriate standards and notes concerning questions to ask. She does this competently.	L16.1	a,b,c,e,h (individual review)	
I then question the witness on C's progress towards her NVQ and on S's effectiveness. The witness confirms that her candidate is making progress and gives examples of her performance as a reliable, consistent and helpful assessor.			
10:00: I observe S assessing with C, then giving her feedback on her performance.			Witness testimony
S is encouraging, answers C's questions appropriately and proceeds to observe her cleaning, servicing and carrying out routine maintenance on three different floors.			Question and answer

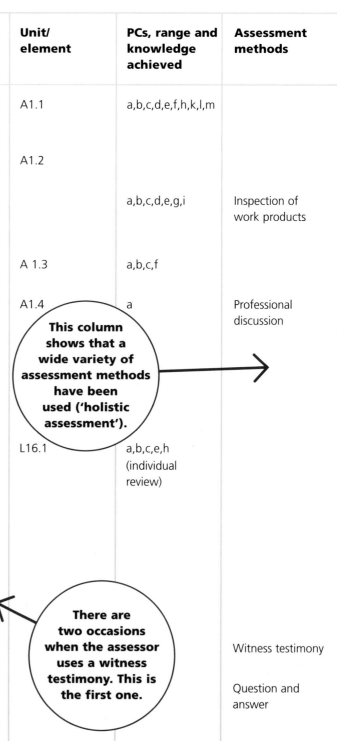

This column shows that a wide variety of assessment methods have been used ('holistic assessment').

There are two occasions when the assessor uses a witness testimony. This is the first one.

She stands close enough to C to see what she is doing, but ensures that she is not disruptive, She has the standards open in front of her and takes notes.

C discovers a fault with an electric cable and shows this to S who then questions her on health and safety and relevant reporting procedures.

12:00: I question C on her own about her NVQ. She is very positive about S, saying that assessment of, and feedback on, her performance have helped her to progress at just the right pace.

I question C about the appeals process, but she says she doesn't know what it is and tells me she would consult her line manager if she had problems with her NVQ. There is no information in her portfolio concerning appeals.

12:20: I observe S giving C feedback on the morning's assessment.

S is very positive about C's performance and takes account of her nerves. She gives C specific instances of occasions when she has proved her competence, including her use of witness testimony and APA. She confirms a time and date for their next assessment and gives C advice on how to prepare her portfolio.

S reviews C's progress to date and they agree a plan of action for the completion of her award. S records key action points and confirms the date of their next assessment in a week's time.

S checks her records, makes sure that they are signed by both her and C, and that they are dated correctly.

Feedback given by BH to SC on her assessment practice

S had an excellent relationship with her candidate, as demonstrated through her sensitive handling of C, who was very nervous.

I felt that S used the right mix of assessment methods and amount of evidence to confirm C's competence.

Although S told me she had explained the appeals procedure to C at induction, I explained that, as there was no evidence of this, she could not achieve the performance criteria and knowledge relevant to appeals and grievance procedures. However, I recommended that she address this as a matter of urgency within her centre at the next team meeting. I explained that by doing so she would produce further evidence of her competence towards A1.4. We agreed to cover this during my assessment of her work with her second candidate.

I concluded by saying that this was an example of excellent assessment practice and I confirmed with S that she had met the standards indicated.

Verbal witness testimony

Observation

Here's the second example of a witness testimony.

This describes how the candidate assessor fails to achieve the standard and how the assessor deals with it.

This statement confirms the candidate's achievement.

These dates may sometimes be different, so it's important to keep a record of both.

Assessor's signature

Candidate's signature

Date of assessment decision

Date

Here are some points to bear in mind when writing reports:

- Use short, clear sentences and simple language so that anyone else reading it can easily understand how you've reached your assessment decisions.

- Think in terms of describing what you've seen and heard during your assessment visit.

- Give timings, particularly if you are there for any length of time.

- Give real examples of the things you've seen your candidate do or of what they've said, to back up the judgements you make.

- Don't just repeat what's in the standards: describe what your candidate does, says and shows you.

- Make sure everything is signed and dated.

- Remember to include your feedback to the candidate, including further action they may need to take.

Giving feedback on performance

An important stage in the learning process is giving learners feedback on their performance and on the assessment decisions you have made. Effective feedback provides the basis for adjusting performance and planning the learner's next steps, and enables you to update the assessment plan. You should use feedback to help you revise learning targets, and to plan for future learning and development needs as necessary.

What the standards say

Element A1.3   Provide feedback and support to candidates on assessment decisions

Assessors need to:

- give candidates feedback at an appropriate time and place.

- give candidates feedback in a constructive and encouraging way, which meets their needs and is appropriate to their level of confidence.

- clearly explain your assessment decisions about whether candidates' evidence of competence is good enough.

- advise candidates who cannot prove their competence how to develop the necessary skills or provide more evidence.

- encourage candidates to get advice on your assessment decisions.

- identify and agree the next steps in the assessment process and how candidates will achieve these.

- follow the agreed complaints and appeals procedures if candidates disagree with your assessment decisions.

Learners need feedback on their performance after every review or assessment visit. Here are some occasions when feedback is needed, and what to do:

Feedback is needed when ...	What to do
the learner's evidence does not meet the standard	Give feedback on the areas where their evidence has not met the standards and the reasons why.
	Tell them exactly what they need to do to succeed next time.
the learner needs further development or training	Revise learning targets to reflect this – allow more time, for example.
	Specify and record the methods by which this is to be provided in the learner's training plan or ILP.
	Liaise with the appropriate people (training staff, or the learner's supervisor, for example) and arrange for suitable development to take place.
	Reschedule assessment visits to allow development to take place.
the learner needs support to achieve their targets	Be clear about the kind of support needed – mentoring? coaching? specialist help?
	Specify and record the methods by which this is to be provided in the learner's training plan or ILP if appropriate.
	Liaise with the appropriate people (training or workplace staff, for example) and arrange for suitable support.
	Reschedule assessment visits if necessary.
the learner achieves the standards	Tell them how they did this by going through your observations and/or their evidence and explaining how what they did meets the standards.
	Praise them for their efforts where they perform particularly well – for example, where performance goes beyond the requirements of the standards.

Setting targets

The A1 standards say that assessors need to 'give candidates advice, when they cannot prove their competence, on how they can develop the necessary skills or provide more evidence'.

You also need to know 'how to give constructive feedback on existing levels of competence and what candidates need to do to be fully competent'.

If learners fail to reach the standards, your job is to advise them how to develop skills and provide more evidence. In practice, this means:

- advising on learning targets
- being involved in planning how to achieve these
- modifying learning targets as a result of any progress reviews and assessments you carry out.

SMART targets

You can use the 'SMART' acronym to help you set effective learning targets. When setting targets, ask:

are they...

> **S**pecific? They define clearly what is to be done

> **M**easurable? You are able to measure whether or not they have been achieved

> **A**chievable? They are realistic and the learner can achieve them

> **R**elevant? They are worth doing and relevant to the standards

> **T**ime bound? The target contains a time limit.

The best targets are always 'SMART*ER*'. They are also:

> **E**njoyable and

> **R**ewarding.

An example of a SMART target might be: 'Plan three ILPs with learners, containing learning targets, learning methods, resources, assessment methods and timescales by the first week in March.'

Self-check

The following questionnaire will help you identify areas where you may need further help with assessing and reaching a judgement.

Do you...	Yes	no
Plan assessment activities with learners?	☐	☐
Use a variety of assessment methods, and can you justify their use?	☐	☐
Use criteria concerning the validity, authenticity, currency and sufficiency of evidence when reaching a judgement?	☐	☐
Feel confident that you make safe and reliable judgements? (If you answer yes, can you prove it?)	☐	☐
Give constructive feedback to learners?	☐	☐
Use feedback on performance to plan learning?	☐	☐

You are aiming to answer yes in all cases. Where you have answered no, talk to your internal verifier about what action to take.

Contributing to quality assurance

An important part of your role as an assessor is contributing to your centre's quality-assurance processes. This isn't something that happens just to satisfy your internal verifier or the awarding body: it is fundamental to ensuring that standards of assessment are maintained and improved upon over time.

The main ways in which you must contribute to quality assurance are by:

- attending team meetings regularly
- contributing to standardisation meetings
- keeping up to date with professional practice.

What the standards say

Element A1.4   Contribute to the internal quality-assurance process

Assessors need to:

- ensure that assessment records are accurate and up to date, and can be followed by an audit.

- contribute to standardisation arrangements so that your assessment decisions are line with others'.

- give accurate and timely information on assessments.

- contribute to the agreed quality-assurance process.

Taking part in meetings

Assessors need to play an *active* part in both team and standardisation meetings. The main point of meetings such as these is to standardise assessment practice among you and your colleagues so that all assessment decisions are applied consistently.

Team meetings are about sharing assessment practice and identifying and solving problems within the centre or your occupational sector.

Standardisation meetings involve looking in depth at particular units or elements within a specific scheme, to identify the evidence produced by the candidates and the assessment methods used. This enables assessors and internal verifiers to determine:

- what evidence they expect learners to produce to meet the particular standards in question
- the best methods to use when assessing this part of the standards
- that all assessors are asking for similar things and are assessing with the same rigour across all candidates.

An internal verifier will set the agenda and lead these meetings, and take responsibility for distributing minutes of any decisions made or changes to assessment practice to team members.

You can play an active part in meetings by:

- being prepared to explain the basis for your assessment decisions and to modify your assessment practice whenever necessary

- keeping a note of any difficulties you have had in making assessment decisions as you assess, and sharing these

- referring any difficulties to your internal verifier, such as issues to do with the learner being competent or 'not yet competent'. (He or she will raise these at meetings and will also pass on any unresolved problems to the awarding body for clarification.)

- being proactive about asking for items to be included on the agenda.

Continuing professional development (CPD)

As a requirement of you assessing NVQs, you must undertake annual CPD. This will keep you up to date with current practice, and is a vital way in which you can contribute to the quality of assessment within your centre. You need to think in terms of:

- maintaining your professional competence within the sector for which you are an assessor.

- keeping up to date with assessment practice.

Maintaining your professional competence

This involves proving that your competence has been maintained or enhanced by:

- attending training courses

- undertaking research, using the Internet or other publications, for example

- joining professional bodies

- subscribing to professional and/or trade journals

- joining local groups such as chambers of commerce.

Keeping up to date

This means:

- proving that you are operating to the A1 occupational standard and within the NVQ Code of Practice. (This could include planning to update your assessor award to the new A units or the Certificate in Review and Assessment of Learning if necessary.)

- making sure that your occupational competence and experience are in line with your sector's relevant assessment strategies

- knowing your sector's occupational standards.

Everything in the list above could be called *intentional* learning. You probably carry out a great deal of *unintentional* learning such as browsing the Internet, and reading books or newspaper articles, all of which could be relevant to your professional development. You need to be aware of occasions such as these and keep a record of them. Any records you keep need to show:

- what you did

- dates and times

- what you learned

- reflection from you on how the experience confirms or has changed your professional practice.

Have a word with your internal verifier about arranging training or further opportunities if you need help.

Remember...

CPD is your responsibility. With this in mind, you need to make it your business to contact your awarding body and find out about any changes to standards and assessment strategies. You may also wish to talk to your internal verifier or manager about your own career progression and find out more about the qualifications available.

The NVQ Code of Practice

The practices and procedures you have met in this section are requirements for all assessors, and are set out in the Code of Practice. If you actively contribute to assuring quality, you are unlikely to encounter problems with measuring your performance against the criteria it contains.

It is worth noting that non-compliance in assessment leads to the following sanctions:

Example of non-compliance   **Sanction**

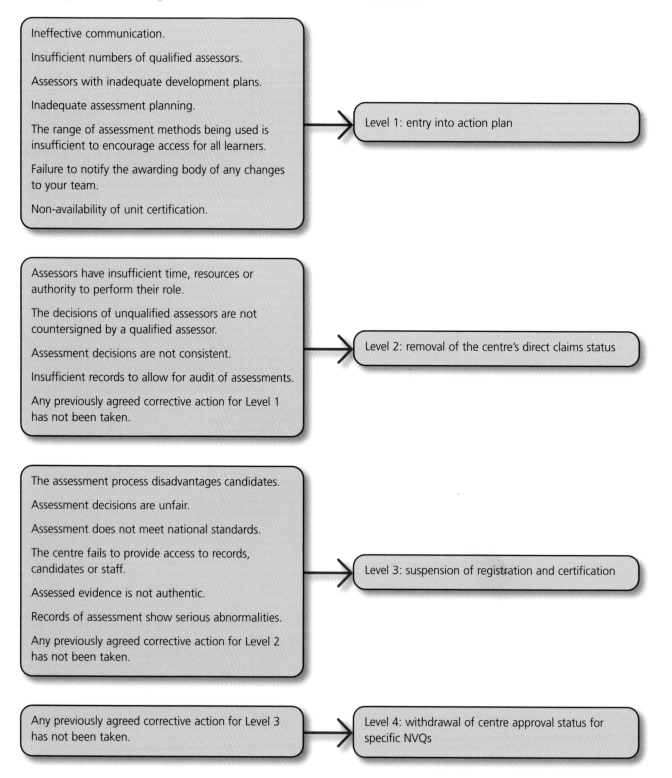

Ineffective communication.

Insufficient numbers of qualified assessors.

Assessors with inadequate development plans.

Inadequate assessment planning.

The range of assessment methods being used is insufficient to encourage access for all learners.

Failure to notify the awarding body of any changes to your team.

Non-availability of unit certification.

> Level 1: entry into action plan

Assessors have insufficient time, resources or authority to perform their role.

The decisions of unqualified assessors are not countersigned by a qualified assessor.

Assessment decisions are not consistent.

Insufficient records to allow for audit of assessments.

Any previously agreed corrective action for Level 1 has not been taken.

> Level 2: removal of the centre's direct claims status

The assessment process disadvantages candidates.

Assessment decisions are unfair.

Assessment does not meet national standards.

The centre fails to provide access to records, candidates or staff.

Assessed evidence is not authentic.

Records of assessment show serious abnormalities.

Any previously agreed corrective action for Level 2 has not been taken.

> Level 3: suspension of registration and certification

Any previously agreed corrective action for Level 3 has not been taken.

> Level 4: withdrawal of centre approval status for specific NVQs

Self-check

The following questionnaire will help you gauge the extent to which you are taking an active part in assuring quality within your centre.

As an assessor...	Yes	no
Do you take part in team meetings with other assessors within the sector for which you are an assessor?	☐	☐
Do you take an *active* part in these meetings – for example, by sharing good and bad practice with other assessors?	☐	☐
Do you hold a current assessor qualification (such as A1/A2 or D32/33), or are you working towards one?	☐	☐
Are you *currently* occupationally competent, and can you prove it?	☐	☐
Do you regularly review and evaluate your own assessment performance?	☐	☐
Do you take part in standardisation meetings?	☐	☐
Do you standardise your own practice as a result?	☐	☐
Do you know the standards and assessment strategies in the qualifications for which you are assessing?	☐	☐
Are you up to date with your centre's and the awarding body's procedures and documentation?	☐	☐
Do you evaluate the delivery of your assessments and make recommendations for improving systems and procedures?	☐	☐
Do you take part in CPD and/or training activities such as staff training days?	☐	☐

If you answered no to any of the above, have a word with your internal verifier about steps you can take to contribute fully to the QA process in the area(s) in question.

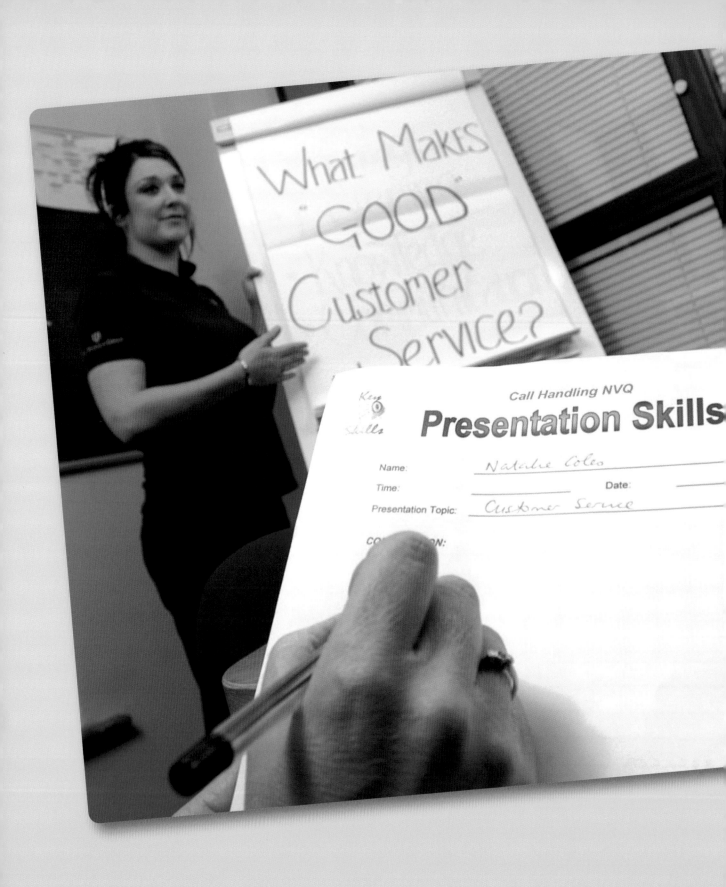

3 Keeping records

It's vital to keep records at each stage of the assessment process, as it ensures that the process you use is:

- ■ ***transparent*** – *everyone can see the assessment decisions and the basis on which they are made*

- ■ ***traceable*** – *those who need to can track progress or follow an 'audit trail' to see how assessment decisions are reached.*

Assessment records are important sources of information for the internal verifier, and can help contribute to improvements in practice and procedures.

Your awarding body will have specific documents that you are required to fill in. Some suggestions for what to use and when are on the next two pages.

Record	When to use it	What it contains	Why?
Learner profile	Recruitment	Special assessment requirements Details of the learner's work-place (the main activities and opportunities) and their role A summary of the learner's development needs	You need to be sure that the learner will succeed – this tells you that the learner has been recruited to the right programme
Learner's action plan	Following induction into the NVQ	The units and elements; action needed to achieve them and estimated completion dates	You need an overall plan of what the learner hopes to achieve and how they are going to get there while on the programme
Qualification record sheet	Have this in the front of the learner's portfolio right at the start, so that they can clearly see what they are doing and the key people involved in the assessment process	Name of candidate Award Name of assessor Name of IV List of all the units that the learner will be undertaking within their NVQ, including the optionals Each unit signed and dated by assessor when completed IV signs off when specific units are IV'd	This confirms that the learner has achieved the qualification and that assessment has been completed and verified. It also shows unit certification
Unit summary sheet	On completion of a unit	Signed and dated by IV, assessor and candidate to confirm successful completion of unit	Unit accreditation
Element record sheet	As you assess	Index to link assessment activities to achieved performance criteria, range/scope and knowledge and where assessments and evidence can be located in the portfolio Signature from the learner to confirm that the evidence is theirs Signature and date from the assessor to confirm completion of element	Keeps track of the details of assessment Tells you where to find evidence in the learner's portfolio
Assessment plan	When the learner is starting to operate to the standards	The units/elements to be assessed Details of the activities and evidence to be used The assessment methods to be used Date of review	Confirms with the learner what they need to produce and how they will be assessed

Record	When to use it	What it contains	Why?
Assessor's report	After each assessment activity	A record describing the assessor's assessment activities, using a range of methods against a variety of evidence, and any feedback given to the learner as a result Signed and dated by the assessor and learner (See page 54 for an example of an assessor's report)	Explains how assessment decisions were made and anything the learner needs to do as a result
Review report	To review the progress of the learner within their NVQ process	Identification of what has been achieved and what is left to do. Identification of any development needs Action agreed and target dates	So that the learner knows how they are doing within their award.

Remember…

All assessment documentation must be signed and dated by the assessor and candidate, and 'signed off' by the internal verifier where necessary as a result of sampling.

Self-check

The following checklist will help you audit your existing record keeping.

Answer the following questions:	Yes	no
Do you have records that inform the recruitment process?	☐	☐
Do your records tell you about the learner and their work placement when they join you?	☐	☐
Do your records tell you when the learner is ready to be assessed?	☐	☐
Does each learner have individual assessment plans?	☐	☐
Do your records enable you to keep track of learners' evidence?	☐	☐
Do you actively involve learners in records concerning assessment of their evidence and of their progress?	☐	☐
Do you keep track of individual progress: • at element level? • at unit level?	☐ ☐	☐ ☐
Do your assessors write assessor reports after each assessment activity?	☐	☐
Are all your records signed and dated by the right people at the right time?	☐	☐

If you answered no to any of the above, have a word with your internal or external verifier about what action to take.

4 Getting qualified

If you work within work-based learning and assessment and are thinking about furthering your career by gaining qualifications, then this section will guide you through the different qualifications available and how they fit together. It will explain the purpose and meaning of the various awards and the units within them, and help you choose the most appropriate qualification or award for your needs.

How the qualifications fit together

Here is a diagram of the learning and development cycle. Each stage has associated learning and development units – for example, assessment and verification units (A1, A2, V1 and V2) can be seen under 'Evaluate learning outcomes'.

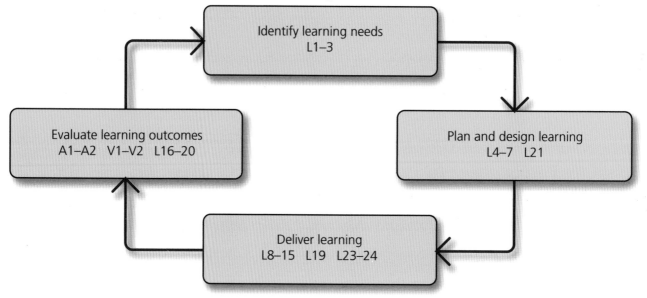

Here are some of the main qualifications:

Award	Title	Units	Aimed at
Certificate	Review and assessment of learning	3 mandatory, (including A1)	NVQ assessors*
Certificate	Initial assessment and support of learners	3 mandatory, 1 optional	NVQ assessors and trainers*
NVQ 3	Learning and development	7 mandatory, 4 optional	Direct trainers
NVQ 3	Direct training and support	6 mandatory, 3 optional	Direct trainers (A1 is an optional unit)*
NVQ 4	Learning and development	8 mandatory, 5 optional	Training managers
NVQ 4	Management of learning and development provision	6 mandatory, 1 optional	Work-based training managers (V1 is an optional unit)*
NVQ 4	Co-ordination of learning and development	6 mandatory, 2 optional	Work-based training co-ordinators (V1 is an optional unit)*
NVQ 5	Learning and development	8 mandatory, 5 optional	Training directors or those responsible for strategy

Those marked with an asterisk * have been designed with the work-based learning sector in mind and are supported by DfES and the LSCs.

The units at a glance

Here are the standards within the assessor and verifier units and what they mean in practice.

Assessors

Unit	Assessors need to...
A1 Assess learners using a range of methods	be occupationally competent and keep up their assessment practice
A1.1 Develop plans for assessing competence	include assessment of prior experience (APE) and achievement (APA) when planning and assessing
	show how their plans are cost effective and realistic, for the candidate and employer as well as for the assessor
	conduct meaningful reviews that inform the resulting assessment plan and thus form part of the overall cycle of learning and development
A1.2 Judge evidence to make assessment decisions	use another person's contribution (witness testimony) towards learners' competence
	use the most effective methods of assessment to judge evidence taken from as many sources as possible
	make sensible use of questioning/professional discussion – *after* the candidate has demonstrated what they know through their performance
A1.3 Provide feedback and support on assessment decisions	record their judgements and explain how they were reached
	advise learners on how to become competent, for example, by talking to other professionals such as the learner's trainer
A1.4 Contribute to the internal quality-assurance process	actively participate in the process – by attending standardisation meetings, for example

Internal verifiers

Unit	Verifiers need to...
V1 Conduct internal quality assurance of the assessment process	be occupationally competent and keep up their verification practice
V1.1 Carry out and evaluate internal assessment and quality- assurance systems	design, implement and evaluate internal verification policies, strategies, systems and procedures develop and implement appropriate staffing structures
V1.2 Support assessors	implement recruitment criteria when selecting assessors manage assessor inductions develop the team and provide ongoing support help assessors to meet ongoing CPD requirements, as required by the relevant assessment strategies
V1.3 Monitor the quality of assessors' performance	sample assessments and observe assessors in action monitor and review learners' progress standardise assessor judgements and the quality of their documentation
V1.4 Meet external quality- assurance requirements	deal with claims submissions and associated administration manage communications and relationships with the awarding body (AB) and the external verifier (EV) make sure AB requirements and assessment strategies are met

External verifiers

Unit	External verifiers need to...
V2 Conduct external quality assurance of the assessment process	be experienced, senior practitioners in the broad occupational area of the standards they will verify
V2.1 Monitor the internal quality- assurance process	monitor a range of different types of centre review the following: assessment methods; administration and recording arrangements; assessor selections, induction and support; standardisation; safety, equality and access arrangements; and internal evaluation
V2.2 Verify the quality of assessment	check staff competence and experience check assessor support and standardisation sample assessor judgements with learners give feedback to centres
V2.3 Provide information, advice and support on the internal quality assurance of assessment processes	provide written and verbal information and support clarify issues and concerns
V2.4 Evaluate the effectiveness of external quality assurance of the assessment process	complete appropriate monitoring reports take part in appropriate updating/standardisation events

Where do your interests lie?

Tick all the items in the left-hand column that interest you. The right-hand column lists qualifications that may be relevant.

I am interested in...	Tick here	You might consider...
Assessing	☐	Unit A1 Certificate in review and assessment of learning
Internal verification	☐	Unit V1
External verification	☐	Unit V2
Delivering learning	☐	Certificate in training and presenting in the workplace Certificate in training and presenting in the workplace Certificate in skills training in the workplace NVQ Level 3 Direct Trainers Award
Helping people with basic skills	☐	Certificate in basic skills development in the workplace. Certificate in basic skills support in the workplace
Mentoring	☐	Certificate in mentoring in the workplace
Coaching	☐	Certificate in coaching in the workplace
Initial assessment	☐	Certificate in initial assessment and support of learners
Designing and managing learning	☐	NVQ Level 4: Management of learning and development provision
Co-ordinating learning	☐	NVQ Level 4: Co-ordination of learning and development

The units contained within the certificates form part of the wider NVQ, so you can progress by adding further units if you wish. Ask your internal verifier, training manager or awarding body for further information if you need to.

Remember...

- If you are already carrying out effective assessment and are actively maintaining your professional development, then by carrying out your job you should be able to achieve units L16, G3, A1: 'Certificate in review and assessment of learning'.

- Unit L16 is entitled 'Monitor and review progress with learners'.

- Unit G3: 'Evaluate and develop own practice' occurs in all the learning and development qualifications.

Further information

Glossary

Adult Learning Inspectorate (ALI) reports on the quality of education and training received by adult learners and young people nationally.

Awarding bodies are responsible for awarding certificates for units and for full NVQs. They use a network of external verifiers to approve centres to deliver NVQs, and to ensure that all centres assess candidates consistently and fairly.

Continuing professional development (CPD) is the process undertaken by trainers, assessors and verifiers to ensure that they are up to date with current professional practice, both within their sector and as part of their training and/or assessment and verification. (As part of the A1 and V1 standards, assessors and verifiers need to demonstrate that they have taken part in CPD.)

Department for Education and Skills (DfES) represents the Government, and sets policy for education and training.

ENTO is the organisation responsible for national occupational standards for learning and development in England, Scotland, Wales and Northern Ireland (see page 77).

Formative assessment is the process of assessing learners to inform and facilitate their progress towards a qualification. The results of formative assessment can be used to help set and revise learning targets and plan what needs to happen next. Formative methods include reviewing.

ILP: Individual learning programme.

Local Enterprise Council (LEC) monitors the delivery and achievement of government-funded training on a local basis, by monitoring and reviewing the performance of providers in Scotland.

Learning Skills Council (LSC) monitors the delivery and achievement of Government-funded training on a local basis, by monitoring and reviewing the performance of providers in England, Wales and Northern Ireland (see page 73).

NVQ: National Vocational Qualification.

Qualifications and Curriculum Authority (QCA) is the accrediting body for England, Wales and Northern Ireland responsible for the development of all academic and vocational qualifications. QCA approves and accredits awarding bodies offering the qualifications, sets common principles and procedures and monitors the awarding bodies.

Scottish Qualifications Authority (SQA): SQA is the accrediting body for Scotland.

Sector Skills Development Agency (SSDA) has been established to underpin the network of sector skills councils and to promote effective working between the sectors.

Sector Skills Council (SSC). There is a network of SSCs (Skills for Business Network) from different occupational sectors, bringing together professional bodies, employers and trade unions to identify the skills needed by those working within particular occupational sectors. They are responsible for delivering Modern Apprenticeship frameworks for their sectors, but do not award NVQs.

Summative assessment takes place when the learner is performing to the standards or targets they are aiming to achieve. Summative methods include testing and observation of performance.

SVQ: Scottish Vocational Qualification.

Who's who in the delivery of NVQs

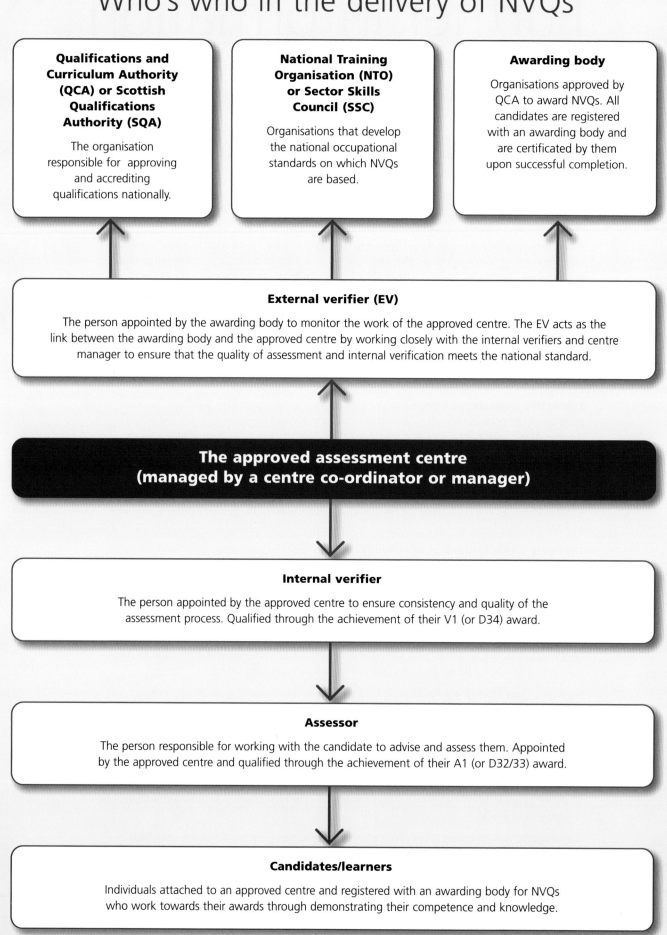

Qualifications and Curriculum Authority (QCA) or Scottish Qualifications Authority (SQA)

The organisation responsible for approving and accrediting qualifications nationally.

National Training Organisation (NTO) or Sector Skills Council (SSC)

Organisations that develop the national occupational standards on which NVQs are based.

Awarding body

Organisations approved by QCA to award NVQs. All candidates are registered with an awarding body and are certificated by them upon successful completion.

External verifier (EV)

The person appointed by the awarding body to monitor the work of the approved centre. The EV acts as the link between the awarding body and the approved centre by working closely with the internal verifiers and centre manager to ensure that the quality of assessment and internal verification meets the national standard.

The approved assessment centre (managed by a centre co-ordinator or manager)

Internal verifier

The person appointed by the approved centre to ensure consistency and quality of the assessment process. Qualified through the achievement of their V1 (or D34) award.

Assessor

The person responsible for working with the candidate to advise and assess them. Appointed by the approved centre and qualified through the achievement of their A1 (or D32/33) award.

Candidates/learners

Individuals attached to an approved centre and registered with an awarding body for NVQs who work towards their awards through demonstrating their competence and knowledge.

About ENTO

ENTO is an independent, self-financing organisation. Since 1988 its purpose has been to develop national vocational standards and qualifications (NVQs) and to provide products and services to support these standards and qualifications.

Our work helps people develop their level of competence and skills, and aims to meet the needs of employees and employers as well as learners. We are also responsible for promoting and monitoring the matrix standard, a quality standard for any organisation that gives information, advice and guidance.

ENTO is unique among national training organisations in that it represents, across all sectors, those whose occupation requires them to deal with people in the workplace. This includes people in the field of information, advice and guidance; learning and development trainers; HR people; recruitment consultants; trade union representatives involved in learning; and health and safety at work practitioners.

Because of this role, the people for whom ENTO standards and qualifications have been developed have a significant influence on the take-up of vocational qualifications throughout the workplace and at all levels. ENTO currently maintains nine suites of National Occupational Standards covering 11 occupational areas, 23 NVQs, 4 Modern Apprenticeships and three suites of non-qualification-based standards.

The Learning Network

The Learning Network is a members-only website run by ENTO for assessors and verifiers across all sectors and disciplines. The network's main aim is to enhance the continuous professional development of assessors and verifiers by equipping them with up-to-date information, providing a forum for discussion and sharing of best practice and the opportunity to influence what is happening in the arena of assessment and verification .

If you would like to join the Learning Network, or find out more, please contact:

Email: info@ento.co.uk

Alternatively, you can click on: www.thelearningnetworkonline.com

Appendix:
an audit tool
for verifiers

This audit tool for verifiers uses a list of questions based on criteria that can be used to benchmark your current practice. Criteria are based on Level 1 and 2 tariff of sanctions from QCA's NVQ Code of Practice (2002). You may need to transfer the questions to several sheets of paper if you wish to develop anything under 'What needs to happen next?' into action points.

Criteria	Yes	Not sure	No
Are our centre aims, policies, assessment practices and responsibilities understood by the team?	☐	☐	☐
Are the internal verification procedures clearly documented?	☐	☐	☐
Do we have effective communications with the awarding body and within our assessment team?	☐	☐	☐
Does our equipment and accommodation comply with health and safety acts?	☐	☐	☐
Do we have enough qualified assessors?	☐	☐	☐
Do all our assessors and IVs have adequate development plans?	☐	☐	☐
Are all our candidates aware of their rights and responsibilities (our appeals procedure, for example)?	☐	☐	☐
Do we have adequate assessment planning with candidates?	☐	☐	☐
Do we record and resolve all candidate queries?	☐	☐	☐
Do we use a sufficient range of assessment methods to encourage access for all candidates?	☐	☐	☐
Do we notify the awarding body of all changes in personnel within the assessment and verification team?	☐	☐	☐
Is unit certification available to all candidates?	☐	☐	☐
Do we monitor and review our procedures? If so, is what we do adequate?	☐	☐	☐
Do our assessors have enough time, resources and/or authority to perform their roles?	☐	☐	☐
Are all assessment decisions made by unqualified assessors countersigned by a qualified assessor?	☐	☐	☐
Are all assessment decisions consistent?	☐	☐	☐
Do we have enough qualified internal verifiers?	☐	☐	☐
Are all decisions made by unqualified IVscountersigned by a qualified IV?	☐	☐	☐
Do we have sufficient records to allow us to audit assessment?	☐	☐	☐

What evidence do we have?	What needs to happen next?